OECD Public Governance Reviews



# Costa Rica: Good Governance, from Process to Results

OECD

BETTER POLICIES FOR BETTER LIVES

This work is published under the responsibility of the Secretary-General of the OECD. The opinions expressed and arguments employed herein do not necessarily reflect the official views of OECD member countries.

This document and any map included herein are without prejudice to the status of or sovereignty over any territory, to the delimitation of international frontiers and boundaries and to the name of any territory, city or area.

**Please cite this publication as:**
OECD (2015), *Costa Rica: Good Governance, from Process to Results*, OECD Public Governance Reviews, OECD Publishing, Paris.
*http://dx.doi.org/10.1787/9789264246997-en*

ISBN 978-92-64-24698-0 (print)
ISBN 978-92-64-24699-7 (PDF)

Series: OECD Public Governance Reviews
ISSN 2219-0406 (print)
ISSN 2219-0414 (online)

The statistical data for Israel are supplied by and under the responsibility of the relevant Israeli authorities. The use of such data by the OECD is without prejudice to the status of the Golan Heights, East Jerusalem and Israeli settlements in the West Bank under the terms of international law.

Corrigenda to OECD publications may be found on line at: *www.oecd.org/about/publishing/corrigenda.htm*.

# *Foreword*

For several decades, Costa Rica has presented a strong track record of political and economic stability. Building on these achievements, the country will need to strengthen its public governance system to address emerging socio-economic challenges, as well as changes within the political system and in the public administration.

In a context of ongoing efforts to improve public governance, the government of Costa Rica has called on the OECD to carry out a Public Governance Review to analyse the strengths and weaknesses of its public administration, and to identify options for increasing the performance of the state in order to ensure more effective and efficient service delivery for all citizens. This Review puts forward ways to improve whole-of-government co-ordination in order to achieve integrated strategic policy outcomes, enrich public policy monitoring and evaluation through the National Evaluation System, and improve annual and multi-annual budgeting and planning. In addition, the Review provides recommendations to strengthen strategic human resources management for its Civil Service Regime, to support integrity policies in public procurement and to improve multi-level governance. As such, the Review seeks to contribute to the country's reform agenda, which aims to sustain important achievements in terms of socio-economic development, and to provide enhanced and sustainable prosperity for its entire population.

Costa Rica is at a turning point: to sustain past achievements, the country's governance system needs to find ways to successfully cope with a changing economy and society. Reforms should include, amongst others, a move from a compliance approach towards a result-oriented focus in different areas such as budget and human resources management; the development of a stronger, shared identity and organisational culture across the public sector; a centre of government that provides clear leadership and vision; and the exploration of new ways of multi-stakeholder engagement in policy-making processes.

The diagnostic and strategic directions presented in this Review were discussed with the Costa Rican authorities over the course of 2014 and have provided input in the public governance area to Costa Rica's National Development Plan for 2015-18.

This Review is part of a series of publications entitled OECD Public Governance Reviews. It was conducted under the auspices of the OECD Public Governance Committee on the basis of its long-standing expertise in public governance reforms and engagement in open government in Members and non-members. The Review seeks to support Costa Rica in its efforts to foster a more effective, efficient, open and inclusive government.

Public Governance Reviews contribute to the work on public administration and management reform of the OECD Public Governance Committee with the support of the Governance Reviews and Partnerships Division of the OECD Public Governance and Territorial Development Directorate. The directorate's mission is to help government at all levels design and implement strategic, evidence-based and innovative policies to strengthen public governance, respond effectively to diverse and disruptive economic, social and environmental challenges and deliver on government's commitments to citizens. The goal is to support countries in building better government systems and implementing policies at both national and regional level that lead to sustainable economic and social development.

# *Acknowledgements*

The OECD Public Governance Reviews are co-ordinated by the Governance Reviews and Partnerships Division, headed by Martin Forst, in the Directorate for Public Governance and Territorial Development, under the responsibility of Rolf Alter, Director, and Luiz De Mello, Deputy Director.

The project was managed by Eva Beuselinck, Policy Analyst in the Governance Reviews and Partnerships Division, who also wrote Chapters 2 and 3. Wilhelmine Brown and Silvia Losada supported the data and information collection process for these chapters. David Goessmann drafted Chapter 1. Chapter 4 was written by Camila Vammalle and Chapter 5 was drafted by Daniel Gerson. Chapter 6 was written by Emma Cantera. Chapter 7 was prepared by Raffaele Trapasso. Administrative and production assistance were provided by Virginie Mendy and Katarzyna Weil. Jennifer Allain and Ciara Muller prepared the manuscript for publication.

This Review would not have been possible without the support of the interlocutors in the Costa Rican government. Special thanks are attributed to the co-ordinating team at the Ministry of Foreign Trade, in particular Marianne Bennett, Adriana González and Raquel Chanto. The Review team also wishes to thank the different participants in the interviews and seminars that took place during the fact-finding mission, including amongst others, representatives from the Ministry of Planning, the Ministry of Finance, the Office of the Comptroller General, the Civil Service Directorate General and the Ministry of the Presidency.

The Review also benefited from insights provided by peer reviewers who participated in the fact-finding mission and contributed to the report and the peer review process:

- Dustin Brown, Deputy Assistant Director for Management, Office of Management and Budget, United States
- Natasha Cray, Public Service Sick Leave Policy, Civil Service HR Division, Department of Public Expenditure and Reform, Ireland
- Orlando García, Director of Monitoring and Evaluation of Public Policies, Colombian National Planning Department, Colombia
- Junghun Kim, Director, Research Group for Government Expenditure, Korea Institute of Public Finance, Korea
- Francisco Sebastián Sánchez Lay, Lawyer for the Citizen Defense and Transparency Commission, Ministry of the General Secretariat of the Presidency, Chile.

The Review process benefited from an interactive policy seminar with Costa Rican stakeholders to discuss the main findings and recommendations, including a meeting with the President of the Republic of Costa Rica and leading ministers in San José in December 2014.

# Table of contents

**Tables**



**Figures**

## Boxes

# Acronyms and abbreviations

| | |
|---|---|
| ADP | Senior Public Management System (Chile)<br>*Sistema de Alta Dirección Pública (Chile)* |
| ANCP | Portuguese National Agency for Public Procurement |
| Caja | Costa Rican Department of Social Security<br>*Caja Costarricense de Seguro Social* |
| CCCI | Cantonal Council for Inter-institutional Co-ordination<br>*Consejo Cantonal de Coordinación Institucional* |
| CGR | Office of the Comptroller General<br>*Contraloría General de la República* |
| CoG | Centre of government |
| CONFIS | Superior Council on Fiscal Policy (Colombia)<br>*Consejo Superior de Política Fiscal (Colombia)* |
| CPI | Corruption Perception Index (Transparency International) |
| CSDG | Civil Service Directorate General |
| CSR | Civil Service Regime |
| DPMPP | Department of Property Management and Public Procurement (Ministry of Finance) |
| GDP | Gross domestic product |
| FDI | Foreign direct investment |
| FOCEVAL | Evaluation Capacity Development in Latin America (German Institute for Development Evaluation) |
| ICE | Costa Rican Institute of Electricity<br>*Instituto Costarricense de Electricidad* |
| IMAS | Joint Social Welfare Institute<br>*Instituto Mixto de Ayuda Social* |
| INTOSAI | International Standards of Supreme Audit Institutions |
| HDI | Human Development Index |
| HRM | Human resources management |
| LAC | Latin America and the Caribbean |
| LOOT | Organic Law governing the Territorial Organisation (Colombia)<br>*Ley Orgánica de Ordenamiento Territorial (Colombia)* |

| | |
|---|---|
| **MEP** | Ministry of Public Education<br>*Ministerio de Educación Pública* |
| **MIDEPLAN** | Ministry of National Planning and Economic Policy<br>*Ministerio de Planificación Nacional y Política Económica* |
| **MNE** | Multinational enterprise |
| **MTEF** | Medium-term expenditure framework |
| **NDP** | National Development Plan |
| **NPEP** | National Public Employment Policy |
| **NPS** | National Planning System |
| **PANI** | National Children's Trust<br>*Patronato Nacional de la Infancia* |
| **PEMANDU** | Performance Management and Delivery Unit (Malaysia) |
| **PISA** | Programme for International Student Assessment (OECD) |
| **SAI** | Supreme audit institution |
| **SICOP** | Costa Rican System of Public Procurement<br>*Sistema Costarricense de Compras Públicas* |
| **SINE** | National Evaluation System<br>*Sistema Nacional de Evaluación* |
| **STAP** | Technical Secretariat of the Budgetary Authority<br>*Secretaría Técnica de la Autoridad Presupuestaria* |
| **UNDP** | United Nations Development Programme |

# Country profile: Costa Rica

| | |
|---|---|
| **Geography, population and living standards** | |
| Area (km$^2$) | 51,100 |
| Population | 4,938,000 (2014) |
| Population density (people per sq. km of land area) | 97 (2014) |
| Urban population | 76% |
| Population growth rate (Annual %) | 1.3% (2014) |
| Total fertility rate | 1.8 children born/woman (2013) |
| Life expectancy | 80 years (2013) |
| Ethnic groups (2011) | - White or mestizo 83.6%<br>- Mulato 6.7%<br>- Indigenous 2.4%<br>- Black of African descent 1.1%<br>- Other 1.1%<br>- None 2.9%<br>- Unspecified 2.2% (2011 est.) |
| **Government** | |
| State structure | Democratic Republic |
| Executive | - President elected by popular vote for a four-year term (No immediate reelection)<br>- The President is simultaneously the head of government and head of state |
| Legislative | Unicameral Parliament (57 seats - Asamblea Legislativa)<br>Four-year term with no immediate reelecion |
| Elections | Last presidential and parlamentary elections held on 2 February 2014 |
| Political situation | The Government is headed by Luis Guillermo Solis Rivera from the *Partido Acción Ciudadana.* This is the first time this party has won the elections. |
| Legal system | Civil law system; Legislative acts can be appeled to the Constitutional Chamber of the Supreme Court. |
| Administrative-territorial structure | Costa Rica is divided into 7 provinces, which are subdivided into 81 cantons or municipalities. These are further divided in 421 districts. |

*Source:* World Bank database; CIA factbook; Costa Rican Constitution.

# Executive summary

Costa Rica stands out in the region for its political and economic stability. In 1949, the country dissolved its armed forces and adopted a new Constitution. The Constitution fostered broad-based access to education and healthcare, a robust system of checks and balances, and a strong rule of law. Sound mechanisms to oversee state action as well as to protect and guarantee human and democratic rights were progressively installed. Relatively stable, long-term economic growth has allowed for important investments in basic social services, while a good endowment of human capital and natural amenities has further contributed to socio-economic progress. The average life expectancy at birth of Costa Ricans is significantly higher than in other Latin American countries and Costa Rica made important progress on the Human Development Index.

But rising socio-economic challenges and changes in the political system and in the administration are putting pressure on the country's governance mechanisms and constrain Costa Rica's aspirations for enhanced and sustainable prosperity for its entire population. These challenges include a fragmented public administration with limited steering capacity by the centre of government, a large share of the budget falling outside the budgetary preparatory process headed by the Ministry of Finance, fiscal sustainability severely under pressure, and regional disparities as well as rising inequalities.

Whereas important efforts have been made to further modernise the country's public administration, progress should be made in different areas in order to make Costa Rica a forward-looking, resilient state:

- The centre of government's leadership and co-ordination remain relatively weak in comparison to OECD standards, due to high political and public sector fragmentation, in addition to some capacity constraints at both technical and strategic level.
- Costa Rica's monitoring and evaluation culture is still essentially process-oriented, available performance information is not strategically used often enough, and there is limited policy evaluation capacity across the public sector. A shift towards a result-oriented culture needs to be fostered.
- The country has reached the limits of what traditional budget systems can achieve. Challenges include, amongst others, high budget rigidities, a lack of fiscal space and weak fiscal constraints. In addition, a large share of the budget falls outside the budgetary process, headed by the Ministry of Finance.
- The current human resources management in the public sector lacks reliable workforce data. Merit-based hiring has been widely adopted, but the compensation system is overly complex, leading to pay distortions. The current Civil Service Regime lacks effective workforce planning tools and competency management has not been adopted across the public sector yet.

- The country's public procurement system is characterised by a strong *ex ante* control. The system is fragmented, with several digital platforms and different thresholds to carry out different procedures across institutions. Overall, procurement officials adopt a compliance-based approach, and there is no professionalised procurement workforce.
- Although the constitutional reform of 2001 allocated more power to sub-national levels, this still needs to be implemented: the role of municipalities in service delivery remains limited for the time being.

This Review advises the government of Costa Rica on ways to address these challenges and has identified priority areas for action to strengthen the quality and efficiency of public institutions.

To **improve whole-of-government co-ordination** in order to achieve integrated strategic outcomes, the Review recommends to:

- enhance the strategic role of the Ministry of the Presidency
- invest in capacity building for key centre of government institutions
- develop a framework for steering and co-ordinating the institutionally decentralised sector, including appropriate co-ordination instruments, a strategy to rationalise the institutionally decentralised sector and a clear definition of agency performance
- develop multi-stakeholder follow-up mechanisms of the National Development Plan
- develop and adopt consultation principles throughout the public sector.

To **enhance public policy monitoring and evaluation**, the Review recommends to:

- promote a result-oriented monitoring and evaluation culture across the public sector
- develop a balanced approach between "accountability" and "learning" objectives, to minimise the risks of performance overrating or unambitious goal setting, and to safeguard the opportunity to learn from occasional weak performance and policy failures
- focus on strengthening the capacity of all actors of the monitoring and evaluation chain
- provide incentives to actors involved in the use of monitoring and evaluation data, such as allowing policy goals to be revised where needed and rewarding goal achievement
- allow for gradual development of the monitoring and evaluation system, with a focus on getting the basics right and subsequently the identification of more ambitious goals, such as linking the monitoring and evaluation system to the budget cycle or risk assessments
- promote citizen and stakeholder participation in the evaluation process.

In order to **strengthen the budget framework for strategic planning**, it is recommended to:

- create and ensure fiscal space through a review of budgetary earmarks, strengthened planning, spending reviews, sunset clauses for new initiatives and the use of performance incentives
- align the institutionally decentralised sector with government priorities through strengthened accountability, basic conditionalities for budgetary transfers and high-level policy co-ordination
- ensure fiscal sustainability through a renewed compliance with constitutional requirements, a comprehensive medium-term fiscal and expenditure framework, fiscal rules monitoring, fiscal examination of new legislation and a single centrally controlled treasury fund.

To **support human resources management**, the Review recommends to:

- improve the quality and consistency of workforce data to improve transparency and enable more informed decision making
- evolve towards a more merit-based, simplified and financially sustainable compensation system, including non-monetary incentives
- introduce competency management to enable effective and coherent workforce planning, recruitment and selection, mobility and employee development
- strengthen performance management, to link the investment in staff to better service outcomes
- build institutional and individual leadership.

To **support integrity policies and public procurement**, the Review recommends to:

- agree on a single procurement platform that covers the whole public sector (including autonomous entities) and the entire procurement cycle
- consider the creation of a public procurement authority to set a national procurement vision and strategy
- allow a gradual reduction of *ex ante* controls, combined with improved internal control and risk management systems
- increase the transparency of the procurement process, including the application of a unique set of thresholds for procurement procedures and the development of guidelines for contract clustering
- enhance the professionalisation of the procurement workforce through the provision of training and adequate incentives to attract the right people
- enhance stakeholder involvement through the different stages of the procurement process.

For Costa Rica to **improve its multi-level governance**, the Review recommends to:

- introduce flexibility in the governance system to help tailor policies to places and provide the possibility to experiment with different governance mechanisms
- create a network of community agents providing local government with capacity building, including support on how to deal with the institutionally decentralised sector

- use contracts to facilitate the functional relation between the central government and municipalities.

Costa Rica is at a turning point. In order to sustain the important achievements of the past, the country's governance system needs to shift gear and mirror the changing economy and society. This Review provides input for a reform process that can foster a more efficient, effective and accountable public administration with a clear focus on delivering results and improving the well-being of the entire population.

# Assessment and recommendations

## Contextualising the need for public governance reforms

The Republic of Costa Rica is one of the most stable democracies of the Americas. The Political Constitution of the Republic of 1949, including the abolishment of the army, fostered the provision of broad-based access to education and healthcare, as well as the creation of a robust system of checks and balances with a particularly strong position of the Comptroller General and a strong rule of law. Relatively stable, long-term economic growth has contributed to an important investment in basic social services, while a good endowment of human capital and natural amenities has further contributed to socio-economic progress.

Fragmentation of the political system and the public administration, next to an increasing number of socio-economic challenges, are putting pressure on the country's governance mechanisms and have resulted in decreasing trust in public institutions. Specific challenges include the following observations:

- The country has a fragmented public administration, which is characterised by an important number of subsidiary bodies of central government ministries and a large institutionally decentralised sector (e.g. semi-autonomous and autonomous bodies, state- and non-state-owned enterprises), with limited steering capacity by the centre of government and limited accountability mechanisms.
- A large share of the budget (about 50% of total consolidated general government spending, managed by the institutionally decentralised sector) falls outside the budget preparatory process headed by the Ministry of Finance and is excluded from direct scrutiny by the Legislative Assembly.
- Fiscal sustainability is under pressure, with one of the largest (and rising) deficits in the region, a low tax-to-GDP ratio in comparison with regional and OECD standards, and rising debt figures since the global financial crisis (currently about 36% of GDP*; IMF 2015 data), combined with a very high level of budgetary earmarking at constitutional and legal level (about 95% of central government expenditures are pre-assigned) – the latter being high even from a Latin American comparative perspective.
- Regional disparities in economic and social development exist across the country and, despite an expanding middle class, rising inequalities (i.e. rising Gini coefficient).

At Costa Rica's request, this Review advices on the "how" of effective governance reform in support of the government's strategic objectives to enhance centre of government co-ordination capacity, to improve monitoring and evaluation, to link the budget to strategic planning, to promote better human resources management and

* IMF (2015), "Costa Rica", *IMF Country Report*, No. 15/29, www.imf.org/external/pubs/ft/scr/2015/cr1529.pdf.

integrity policies in procurement, and to achieve integrated national and regional development outcomes. As such, the Review seeks to contribute to Costa Rica's reform agenda which aims to sustain important historical achievements in terms of socio-economic development, and to provide enhanced and sustainable prosperity for its entire population.

## Enhancing centre of government co-ordination capacity

The centre of government (CoG) in Costa Rica – composed of the Ministry of the Presidency, the Ministry of National Planning and Economic Policy (Ministerio de Planificación Nacional y Política Económica, MIDEPLAN), the Ministry of Finance and the Budgetary Authority – faces similar challenges to the CoG of many OECD Members. In a difficult fiscal context, CoGs need to ensure vision, leadership and innovation. In Costa Rica, this is all the more difficult as the country is confronted with high levels of political and public sector fragmentation (i.e. a particularly important institutionally decentralised sector), as well as some capacity constraints at both technical and strategic level, all putting pressure on the strategic policy-making capacity of the state and its service delivery capacity.

In order to strengthen the CoG's strategic capacity, the following recommendations can be formulated:

- Enhancement of the strategic role of the Ministry of the Presidency to support the quality of the decision-making process of the Council of Ministers, by reviewing agenda proposals on different dimensions. Such a review could cover a procedural check, a coherence check with the government's programme, a consultation check of relevant stakeholders, a legal conformity check, a regulatory standards check and a costing check. The balance between administrative and strategic support assured by the Ministry of the Presidency could subsequently be reflected in its organisational chart, fostering stability across different government periods, in order to build and preserve capacity.
- Structural investment in CoG capacity building, given the substantial turnover within CoG institutions in the past (reflecting turnover in the Costa Rican public sector in general, in line with the political cycle) and the substantial challenges for successful CoG co-ordination the country is facing. Primary beneficiaries for such training would be the Ministry of the Presidency and MIDEPLAN, and could cover technical training, as well as the development of soft skills, like negotiation and communication skills.
- Development of a clear policy on CoG steering of the institutionally decentralised sector, with a clear set of steering, co-ordination and control mechanisms; a strategy to gradually rationalise the institutionally decentralised sector in order to strengthen the CoG steering and co-ordination capacity towards the institutionally decentralised sector; and univocal guidelines regarding the creation of agencies. A clear definition of agency performance (i.e. going beyond quantitative indicators, and also addressing quality, effectiveness, equal access and responsiveness) and the development of a policy regarding the use of performance targets (to be used as an opportunity to improve communication, exchange, negotiation and mutual learning) are instrumental as well.
- Development of multi-stakeholder follow-up mechanisms of the National Development Plan, so as to not lose momentum and strengthen the ownership of

the plan. The government has made substantial efforts to strengthen the participatory dimension of the development of the National Development Plan. These efforts should now be sustained throughout its implementation.

- Development of consultation principles to be adopted throughout the public sector, to ensure that citizen participation goes beyond the initial development of the National Development Plan. Such consultation principles would help policy makers to make the right judgments about when, with whom and how to consult.

## Monitoring and evaluation as a policy tool to become result oriented

Sound monitoring and evaluation of the performance and progress of public interventions implies the capacity to detect policy challenges, define adjustments to facilitate decision-making processes, feed strategic information into the decision-making process, and communicate in a timely manner to decision makers in order to achieve the expected goals of public interventions. In addition, strong monitoring and evaluation can foster transparency and accountability, and provide stakeholders with information regarding progress in the accomplishment of government goals and commitments. While Costa Rica formally established a national monitoring and evaluation system about two decades ago, it still has not made the shift from a process-oriented towards a result-oriented monitoring and evaluation culture. The country faces challenges in using performance information strategically, in fine-tuning the coherence of its budget and policy cycle, and of policy evaluation capacity constraints across the public sector.

To foster the result-oriented focus of its current monitoring and evaluation system, Costa Rica should:

- Promote the use of a balanced set of result criteria across the public sector, not only focusing on criteria like efficiency, effectiveness and economy, but also incorporating criteria like quality, equal access and responsiveness.
- Develop a balanced approach between "accountability" and "learning" objectives of the evaluation system. A greater emphasis on, and higher visibility of, result achievement can provoke counterproductive incentives to overrate performance and/or to focus on targets which are easy to achieve (i.e. lack of ambitious goal setting). Moreover, it risks suppressing the opportunity to learn from occasional weak performance and policy failures, if no room is left to make mistakes and learn from them. The monitoring and evaluation system should strike a balance between a focus on goal achievement, on the one hand, and on understanding the "why" of good or bad performance, on the other hand.
- Focus on strengthening the capacity of all actors of the monitoring and evaluation chain. This implies, amongst others, a strategic approach across government to capacity development for data collection, data analysis, and reporting, communication and use of data. It is important to acknowledge that a supply of performance data does not imply that people know how to analyse and interpret the data and, subsequently, how to use the data. In addition, clear roles and responsibilities have to be assigned to different actors (i.e. suppliers and users of performance information). In order to ensure strategic resource allocation, it is important to develop a clear view on hierarchy of goals, and an appropriate timing and frequency for data collection and analysis which allows for proper feedback loops.

- Provide incentives to actors involved in the use of monitoring and evaluation data, i.e. empowerment to act upon performance information. Such empowerment could be linked to the ability to revise policy priorities and performance goals, identify corrective actions to address observed problems, including budgetary reallocation where needed, reward goal achievement, etc. Whereas roping in the institutionally decentralised sector is important to ensure achievement of strategic goals across government, this requires a specific set of incentives, given its level of autonomy.
- Allow for gradual development of the monitoring and evaluation system. Getting the system "up and running" (i.e. design the process, define the goals, identify the available monitoring and evaluation tools, detect capacity development needs, etc.) is a first step. Subsequently, the government can identify "systemic goals" of the monitoring and evaluation system, which could gradually become more ambitious, e.g. measurement of performance, identification of corrective measures, informing the budgetary process, incorporating risk assessments, etc. Each of these goals requires substantial resources and time to achieve. A particular point of attention is the development of a strategy on how to address cross-institutional goals. Such cross-institutional policy objectives tend to be numerous, whereas strengthening monitoring and evaluation of individual institutions risks reinforcing a silo-based approach.
- Promote citizen and stakeholder participation in the evaluation process, through polls or focus groups carried out periodically, to explore the public's perception of government achievements.

## Strengthening the budget framework for strategic planning

Costa Rica has made the most of traditional budget systems, and has reached the limits of what these traditional systems can achieve. It now needs to take a step forward and look at modern budgeting practices in order to secure sustainable social and economic development. The country has taken steps towards programme budgeting and a medium-term expenditure framework, but it still encounters substantial challenges. While the budget process in Costa Rica is well institutionalised and regulated by the Constitution and Budget of the Republic Act, only a share of the budget is discussed by the Legislative Assembly, there is high budget rigidity, lack of fiscal space, weak fiscal constraints and limited budget transparency in terms of readability of available documents. In order to finance new government priorities, Costa Rica runs significant budget deficits, which threaten fiscal sustainability. In addition, the government has a very limited control over the allocation and performance of general government and total public spending, so it is necessary to find a mechanism to monitor the institutionally decentralised public institutions and make sure their plans are coherent with the National Development Plan. Given the limited capacity of the government to reallocate funds from one spending area to another, it is all the more important to improve the efficiency and effectiveness of the use of funds within each spending area, and to reallocate funds from one programme to another within the mandated spending floors. While budget rigidities constrain budget decisions, there is room to improve spending efficiency and prioritisation within the mandated expenditure.

To move beyond a mechanistic budgetary allocation process and develop a sustainable fiscal path, the following actions can be undertaken:

- Create and ensure fiscal space by:
  - Reviewing the formulas of budgetary earmarks, e.g. needs- or population-based, rather than revenue- or GDP-based.
  - Strengthening the planning system with a clear CoG leadership, sector leaders identifying a limited set of medium-term objectives, empowered ministers to carry out resource reallocation, and overall fostering of public accountability of progress.
  - Carrying out spending reviews to identify options for reductions of baseline spending and to reallocate spending, in order to ensure optimal value for money of public spending, being a particular challenge in a context of high budgetary earmarking. Allowing institutions to keep the identified savings and allocate them to new priorities is a good incentive to ensure their co-operation in the identification of possible savings.
  - Envisaging time limits ("sunsets") for new programmes backed by sound evaluations, sufficiently ahead of the sunset date, and/or pay-as-you-go rules by conditioning the allocation of resources to new programmes to the termination or reduction of others by a similar amount.
  - Reinforcing performance-informed budgeting practices, including for the institutionally decentralised sector.
- Align the institutionally decentralised sector with government priorities through:
  - Strengthened accountability, monitoring and evaluation mechanisms and development of a checklist to apply when considering the creation of an institutionally decentralised agency (i.e. addressing relevance, level of autonomy, legal personality, control mechanism, sunset clauses). Such a checklist could also be the basis for a review of the current institutionally decentralised sector.
  - The development of conditionalities associated with budgetary transfers from the central government to the institutionally decentralised sector (e.g. addressing objectives, performance targets, etc.).
  - The creation of a high-level policy co-ordination body, including representatives of the decentralised institutions.
- Ensuring fiscal sustainability by:
  - Reactivating the well-designed constitutional requirements on fiscal discipline (e.g. through a fiscal responsibility law covering fiscal rules regarding revenue, expenditure, budget balance and debt).
  - Developing a comprehensive medium-term fiscal framework, complemented with a medium-term expenditure framework, backed by a system of top-down budgeting which sets aggregate public financial targets and sector ceilings.
  - Clustering the responsibility to issue and monitor the compliance and implementation of fiscal rules within one institution, by either assigning that role to an already existing independent institution or by creating an independent fiscal institution, but with particular attention for the democratic legitimacy of such an institution.

– Adopting tools and procedural rules to make the fiscal examination of permanent legislation more rigorous, in order to make sure that the long-term fiscal cost of legislation is correctly understood and taken into account by the Legislative Assembly when voting it.

– Considering the creation of a single centrally controlled treasury fund for all public revenues and expenditure, including the institutionally decentralised institutions.

## Supporting human resources management

Costa Rica consistently ranks highest in the region on civil service development indicators. But due to the structure of public employment – which is divided into a number of administrative divisions – a new set of modern challenges has emerged. The Constitution of 1949 and the subsequent Civil Service Statue of 1953 established the Civil Service Regime to regulate public employment in the national executive branch, which includes ministries and their subsidiary bodies – a total of 47 entities covering about one-third of public employees. Outside the Civil Service Regime, most public institutions have their own legislation regulating public employment and human resources management (HRM) practices. In addition, collective agreements in various institutions grant employees privileges regarding pay, bonuses, incentives and working hours, which vary from one institution to the next. This myriad of legislation and collective agreements leads to a plurality of HRM systems and policies, which results in significant disparity in the treatment of employees across institutions. The institutionally decentralised entities tend to offer better salaries and benefits, with greater employment flexibility.

The current National Development Plan includes public employment as a priority and recognises the role of effective HRM to strengthen the public institutions of the Costa Rican government. The following reforms will help the country to further capitalise on its current human resource management strengths:

- Improving the quality and consistency of workforce data in Costa Rica is a fundamental step to improve the transparency of the sector and enable more informed HRM decision making. When linked to salary information, it will also help to better manage and control the costs of the workforce, an important challenge Costa Rica is facing.
- Evolving towards a more merit-based, transparent and sustainable compensation system including non-monetary incentives. The current compensation system can be simplified by beginning a gradual transition towards a "single salary" system, meaning an amalgamation of base salary and bonuses and allowances. Any additional payments on top of the base salary need to be universal and made as transparent and simple as possible. This does not need to initially result in a reduction of salary for any staff, and given the legal constraints, it may only be possible to implement this policy for new employees. This means taking a long view (up to 35 years) which therefore increases the urgency to begin. Pay reform should also be linked to broader budget reforms. This, however, would depend upon the development of more strategic HRM frameworks which would emphasise competency-based management, performance management and professional public sector leadership.

- Introducing competency management as a foundation for more strategic human resources management. Using a common competency framework for planning, recruitment and selection, mobility and development will provide Costa Rica with a solid foundation to address its current and future HR needs. Competency management can help to ensure that the civil service of Costa Rica has the range of skills needed to achieve the government's long-term goals. A competency framework enables organisations to better fill competency gaps identified in the workforce planning process while maintaining a high level of objective merit throughout the process. It also supports horizontal and vertical mobility and agility by helping to define common career paths and provides an effective and efficient way of aligning staff development investments with identified organisational requirements.
- Strengthening performance management can play a vital role in linking the individual efforts of employees to larger organisational goals. The focus should be on simplifying the current guidelines and developing managers to implement the new programme. IT platforms can support performance assessment, providing a transparent mechanism to compile and share assessment information. However, the primary focus has to be first and foremost on developing an understandable tool that can be easily applied by managers and staff at all levels of the system with appropriate incentives for good performers. Pay for performance should not be an immediate priority. Instead, consideration should be given to improving the assessment ratings, training managers and staff to use them, and eventually linking them to career development and advancement. Finally, the system would benefit from a clear, transparent and fair policy for under-performers focused first on attempting to develop staff, with eventual dismissal for continued under-performance.
- Building institutional and individual leadership. Costa Rica's central HRM authority is increasingly delegating some of its responsibilities to HRM offices of individual institutions under its authority. Supporting ministries and agencies in an increasingly delegated environment suggests the need to consider new tools and methods. These could include the use of management accountability frameworks, a simplified centralised policy framework, and the use of communication tools and forums to ensure effective dialogue and sharing of best practice experience. Furthermore, the emphasis on management development should include both formal training to close gaps in leadership and management capabilities as well as active learning methods to ensure managers' competencies remain up to date. Leadership and management development activities are most likely to be effective when they are defined as a high priority by the government, and could be guided by a task force of senior managers to ensure their buy-in from the beginning.

## Supporting integrity policies in public procurement

Costa Rica has a long standing tradition of making efforts to achieve proper management of public funds. These go back to 1825 (creation of the Courts of Accounts by Congress), with additional milestones like the creation of the Comptroller's Office in 1950, supplemented with a sound legal framework. Different reforms to strengthen the legal and institutional framework of the country's public procurement system have been carried out in recent years. However, there is a need to further fine-tune procurement-related functions and to increase transparency and accountability. Despite public procurement's impact on the national budget, Costa Rica currently does not benefit from the strategic leverage of the procurement function, as it is perceived as an administrative task. Procurement does not fully achieve its strategic potential due to the lack of a fully cohesive framework, orienting all institutions towards clear priorities and objectives and encouraging public servants to see this function as something more than an administrative checklist.

In order to strengthen the institutional framework and the transparency and accountability of the public procurement process, Costa Rica should:

- Agree on a single procurement platform that covers the whole public sector and the whole procurement cycle, including the institutionally decentralised sector. In order to ensure transparency, provide equal access to information for all suppliers, and promote competition and reinforce supplier trust, the country will need to ensure a proper integration of the multiple existing platforms. This would also require training and raising the awareness of public officials. The platform could also establish a system of red flags or mechanisms to track decisions and enable the identification of irregularities and potential corruption cases in public procurement.
- Consider the creation of a public procurement authority, within the limits of the Constitution, to set a national procurement vision, and set procurement priorities and objectives, including savings and policy objectives such as the promotion of small and medium-sized enterprises, and encourage green procurement and innovation. This public procurement authority could also consolidate goods and services, and promote a more expansive use of framework agreements including the institutionally decentralised sector. An awareness campaign could be undertaken to establish trust and confidence among the different actors on the benefits of a procurement authority.
- Allow a gradual reduction of *ex ante* controls if public entities can demonstrate improvements in internal control and risk management. The Comptroller General will need to monitor and evaluate the quality of internal controls and can start to pilot this possibility on an entity or sector base. In addition, an institutionalised communication network amongst internal control units could be facilitated. This implies a reassessment of the role of the Comptroller General, within its constitutional mandate, implying a review of the continued relevance of its existing assignments and exploration of new ones.
- Roll out of a series of practical measures to increase the transparency of the procurement process, like the application of a unique set of thresholds for procurement procedures, identification through e-procurement tools of good practices for contract clustering, better needs identification and adequate planning, and the development of a system to track decisions and enable the identification of irregularities and potential corruption cases.
- Enhance the professionalisation of the procurement workforce. The country could invest in providing adequate incentives to attract highly qualified officials and updating officials' knowledge and skills on a regular basis to reflect regulatory, management and technological evolutions. This could be boosted by developing a formal job description for procurement officials and introducing a specific code of conduct for them.

- Enhance stakeholder involvement through the different stages of the procurement process. Direct accountability to the public and other stakeholders is a fundamental means of increasing transparency and integrity in decision making.

## Improving multi-level governance

Despite important economic development since the 1970s, Costa Rica displays significant territorial imbalances and a rural-urban split. Municipalities currently represent only about 4% of total general government consolidated expenditure. A constitutional reform of 2001 has formally allocated more power and budget to sub-national levels of government. Yet, the associated budgetary transfer (10%) has not been carried out, municipalities still have a limited range of responsibilities and their work continues to be widely determined by national structures and regulations, due in part to financial and institutional capacity limitations. The reform process has stalled since 2001, and most reforms have remained "on paper". The new government elected in 2014 has put decentralisation and governance among the priorities of its agenda and started working to implement past reforms.

To improve the delivery of services across the territory, and close the urban-rural gap, it is recommended to:

- Use contracts to facilitate the functional relation between the central government and municipalities. The advantage of a contract is that it helps identify a specific task to devolve to a given municipality. It clarifies the scope of the devolved activity and even its timeline, if relevant. Finally, the contract also helps clarify the expected outcome, thus facilitating monitoring and evaluation and contributes to the enhancement of institutional trust (routine).
- Create a network of community agents providing local government with capacity building. In order to promote standardisation and exchange of information, existing cantonal councils for co-ordination could be networked by MIDEPLAN, which would serve as the central hub and would be in charge of training the agents to be sent to municipalities. Agents would provide local mayors with technical information and support to deal with the institutionally decentralised sector. Federations of municipalities may also be involved to connect local experiences and identify good policy practices across municipalities. The councils should involve citizens and non-governmental organisations in the identification of key local assets and economic drivers, which should be taken into account in local development strategies. This may positively affect social capital in the country and help increase trust in the government, since municipalities are the forefront of the public sector.
- Introduce flexibility in the governance system to help tailor policies to places. Costa Rica needs to put in place a governance system that is able to generate a range of policies that adapt to the different features of the communities they intend to serve. This requires flexibility and also the possibility to experiment with different territorial systems. The current regional development network, led by the Presidency of the Republic, may promote territorial experiments in which different governance mechanisms are implemented.

# *Chapter 1.*

# Contextualising public governance in Costa Rica

*This chapter provides an overview of Costa Rica's recent politico-administrative, socio-economic and demographic changes and describes how these are putting pressure on the country's governance mechanisms. Costa Rica's political and economic model has been characterised for decades by high political stability and stable economic growth, allowing the country to perform well on social development deliverables like education and health. However, inequalities are on the rise, important economic pillars like the high-tech industry and tourism have come under pressure, a fragmented public sector is struggling to deliver policies and services effectively, and citizens are increasingly losing trust in public institutions and the political system. This chapter therefore underlines the need to strengthen the country's governance capacity in different areas.*

## The rise of a stable and well-performing country

The Republic of Costa Rica is one of the most stable democracies of the Americas. Free and fair elections, peaceful alternations of power and the guaranty of extensive human and democratic rights have characterised the country's political system for a long time. The establishment of a solid institutional framework has guaranteed social and political stability. Costa Rica as it stands today is built on the Political Constitution of the Republic of 1949. Abolishing the army, the Constitution fostered the creation of a solid basic social welfare system, a robust system of checks and balances, and a strong rule of law.

Strong mechanisms to oversee state action as well as to protect and guarantee human and democratic rights were progressively installed. The constitutional reform of 1989 was instrumental in this respect, by introducing the Constitutional Chamber (*Sala Constitucional*) that has become a protector of peoples' rights. The creation of the position of the Ombudsman in 1992 strengthened the ability of citizens to voice their complaints regarding administrative acts. The Comptroller General Organic Act of 1994 enhanced external control functions over the budget, investment and financial management of the state. In 2012, Costa Rica became a member of the Open Government Partnership, making a strong commitment to openness, transparency and accountability of the state.

Political stability has been supported by overall positive economic growth, despite occasional dips, and by relative monetary stability. According to the World Bank (2014a), Costa Rica's economic growth was 5% on average throughout the 1990s. While slowing down in the 2000s, it remained significantly higher than in other Latin American countries. The average tariff rate declined from over 60% in 1985 to 11.7% in 1995 and 5.9% in 2004 (Ministry of Foreign Trade, 2013), and from the 1990s on free-trade zones were established. Since the 1990s, the relatively open economy has been able to attract large sums of foreign direct investment (FDI), principally in knowledge-intense sectors, creating more and better paid jobs for the growing number of well-educated Costa Ricans. The number of jobs created by FDI rose from 7 758 in the period between 2003 and 2005 to 34 385 between 2009 and 2011 (OECD, 2012). The good endowment of human capital and natural amenities have helped the country diversify its economy.

The Costa Rican political and economic model has historically delivered strong social development with commendable achievements in the areas of education, environmental protection and health. The implementation of social reforms in the period of the late 1940s and the 1950s provided broad-based access to education for Costa Ricans. Illiteracy rates are low (UNICEF, 2013) and investment in education is the highest in Central America (Programa Estado de la Nación, 2014). In the 2009 results of the OECD Programme for International Student Assessment (PISA) that benchmarks skills and knowledge outcomes among 15-year-old students across countries, Costa Rica scored well with respect to the OECD average (OECD, 2011). Costa Rica also offers universal healthcare. Largely due to the considerable spending by the state on different social programmes, the average life expectancy at birth of Costa Ricans is significantly higher than in other Latin American countries, increasing from 66.8 in 1970 to 75.7 in 1990 and 79.7 in 2012 (UNICEF, 2013). Between 1980 and 2012, the country made important progress on the Human Development Index, and is now classified as being in the "high human development" category (UNDP, 2013).

Thanks to the combination of economic growth and public investment in social services, most Costa Rican households have managed to improve their living conditions in the past 20 years (Programa Estado de la Nación, 2014). New economic opportunities created by economic growth as well as the existing social security networks have contributed to social mobility. While the middle class represented 18% of the population in 1992, this percentage had already risen to 31% in 2002 and 40% in 2009 (UNDP, 2014).

## A changing socio-economic reality

Despite the growing middle class, inequalities in Costa Rica are on the rise. While in most Latin American countries inequality in labour earnings fell substantially between 2000 and 2010, Costa Rica saw an opposite trend, which is also reflected in its Gini coefficient, the global measure for income inequality. Between 2001 and 2011, Costa Rica was one of the only Latin American countries of which the Gini coefficient rose (Programa Estado de la Nación, 2013). According to the Programa Estado de la Nación (2014), this development is mostly due to an existing disparity between "new" (i.e. based on manufacturing and the service sector) and "old" (i.e. based on agriculture) economies.

The economic model built on high-tech industry and tourism has come under pressure from regional competitors and growing labour costs. In sectors such as tourism, other countries from Latin America and the Caribbean are gaining importance. Business activities are hindered by poor transport infrastructure, difficulty in accessing finance and from an only moderate capacity to innovate (World Economic Forum, 2013). This is reflected in the 2015 Doing Business statistics of the World Bank (2014b), in which Costa Rica only ranks 83rd (out of 189).

Increasing financial constraints on government expenditures are putting pressure on the Costa Rican welfare state and jeopardise investments in social services. High levels of growth since the 1950s have guaranteed stable public finances which allowed the state to spend a significant amount of money on services to the population. However, Costa Rica's tax revenue as a proportion of its gross domestic product (GDP) has not grown in a manner consistent with the type of public service that the population expects. When compared with the OECD average (34.1% in 2013), total tax revenue (general government) is fairly low (22.40% in 2013) (OECD, 2015). Furthermore, Costa Rica has one of the largest budget deficits in Central America (OECD/IDB, 2014). The central government's deficit reached 5.4% of GDP in 2013, the highest in the past ten years, while the government had the lowest level of fiscal flexibility, with 95% of government expenses that were pre-assigned (Programa Estado de la Nación, 2014).

## Pressure on the political system and the public sector

In addition to the changing socio-economic reality, the political system has come under stress from different sides recently, and the public sector is struggling to deliver policies effectively that meet the expectations of the Costa Rican people. The incoming government is facing a new set of challenges. While the country saw a significant extension of rights and liberties, the "democratisation of the Costa Rican democracy" (Programa Estado de la Nación, 2014) was neither accompanied by a growing public budget and institutional efficiency, nor by stronger accountability mechanisms. The political system is deeply fragmented, conflicts between the different powers of the state are on the rise and the number of social conflicts is growing (ibid.).

As is the case in a great number of OECD Members, people are increasingly losing trust in public institutions and the political system. Levels of trust in government have dropped from 53% to 40% between 2010 and 2014 (Gallup World Poll, n.d.), more than three times the average decline across OECD Members for the same period (45% to 40%). According to the *Latinobarómetro*, support for the political system fell from 67.6% in 2004 to 55.9% in 2012 (Alfaro-Redondo and Seligson, 2012). Between 2008 and 2012, the levels of confidence of the Presidency of the Republic fell from 60% to 43% (ibid.). While the Catholic church ranks as the most trusted institution (64.7%), the political parties and the Legislative Assembly are the institutions with the lowest levels of confidence from the public (31.5% and 37.9% respectively; ibid.). Even though Costa Rica ranks better than other Latin American countries in the Transparency International Corruption Perception Index (CPI), the perception of corruption in Costa Rica has also worsened in the last few years (Transparency International, 2014): from 2010 to 2013, Costa Rica dropped eight positions in the CPI. A key lever for government to build back peoples' trust is strong overall government performance (OECD, 2013). As such, the 2015-18 National Development Plan shows a strong commitment to fight corruption and strengthen transparency, efficiency and overall public performance.

Partly due to relatively weak constitutional powers of the executive, but also due to the shift from a bi-partisan to a more fragmented multi-party system that has taken place over the past decade, the executive experiences a weakened position to put forward its legislative agenda. Members, or groups of members, of congress have a *de facto* veto on legislative initiatives (Government of Costa Rica, 2014). This results in a unicameral Legislative Assembly that has difficulties in taking decisions according to the majorities as foreseen by the Constitution (Presidential Commission on Democratic Governance, 2013), with members of Congress that have significant veto powers but that lack the power to promote their own constructive agenda.

The creation of the Constitutional Chamber (1989) and the enormous increase in the number of constitutional decisions has resulted in a shift in the distribution of power. The Constitutional Chamber (*Sala Constitucional*) has become one of the most powerful public entities increasingly addressing highly political issues and intruding in policy matters formerly resolved by the political branches (Wise, 2010). The Constitutional Chamber can intervene at different stages of the policy-making process. If any act or decision of the administration or of private persons has constitutional relevance in the wider sense, the judges of the Constitutional Chamber can be addressed. Decisions in constitutional matters taken by the Constitutional Chamber are exclusive, not reviewable and are binding precedents, except for the Constitutional Chamber itself (Barker, 2000). Since the Costa Rican Constitution covers a great variety of areas and is broad in its categories, the Constitutional Chamber can be considered a necessary actor in any major public policy decision, especially those involving legal reform (Government of Costa Rica, 2014). In the first two years after the creation of the Constitutional Chamber, the number of cases it had to address increased considerably (Figure 1.1). Nowadays, the Chamber handles over 17 000 cases each year (Constitutional Chamber, 2014).

Figure 1.1. **Number of cases in the Constitutional Chamber**

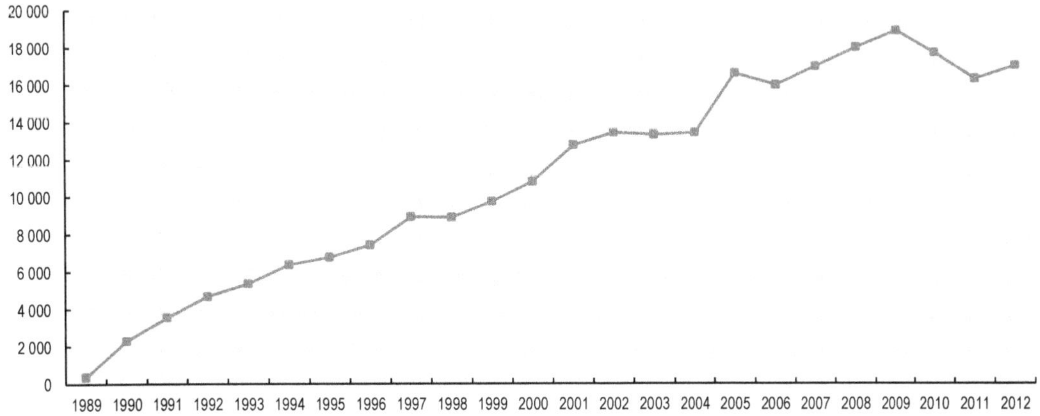


*Source:* Constitutional Chamber (2014), "Number of cases in the Constitutional Chamber 1989-2012", http://sitios.poder-judicial.go.cr/salaconstitucional/estadisticas.htm.

Substantial fragmentation of the public sector puts pressure on the strategic policy-making capacity of the state and its service delivery capacity. While a certain degree of fragmentation is not uncommon in OECD Members (OECD, 2002), this fragmentation poses particular challenges in terms of policy co-ordination. Costa Rica's Constitution not only distinguishes between central government and local government (i.e. "territorially decentralised public sector"), but also establishes the existence of autonomous institutions (Article 188 of the Constitution). As defined in the Costa Rica Public Sector Organigram (Ministry of National Planning and Economic Policy, 2013), the "institutionally decentralised sector" (as opposed to ministries and their subsidiary bodies) encompasses these autonomous institutions, and distinguishes between autonomous institutions and their subsidiary bodies, semi-autonomous institutions, state-owned and non-state-owned public enterprises and non-state public entities that collaborate in the satisfaction of the public interest.

The first entities of the institutionally decentralised sector were created in the 1940s as autonomous institutions with a mandate of policy making as well as service delivery such as health, energy and education. Examples include the Costa Rican Department of Social Security (*Caja Costarricense de Seguro Social* created in 1943), the Costa Rican Electricity Institute (*Instituto Costarricense de Electricidad* created in 1949) and a series of tertiary education colleges created in the 1940s. The creation of many of these was deeply connected to state interventionism in the economy and the import-substitution model. In terms of steering mechanism, these public institutions often dispose of boards of directors that provide both policy and managerial guidance.

From the 1970s onwards, a new wave of creating public institutions is observable, quantitatively and qualitatively different from the past. For instance, between 1991 and 2010 no less than 60 subsidiary bodies of central government ministries were established. These subsidiary bodies primarily represent "policy implementation shortcuts" to attain greater administrative and budgetary flexibility (Government of Costa Rica, 2014).

The budget of the (territorially and institutionally) decentralised sector – approximately 50% of the general government consolidated spending – falls outside the budget process headed by the Ministry of Finance, and is rather supervised (i.e. compliance check) by the Comptroller General (*Contraloría General de la*

*República*). The Comptroller General operates as an auxiliary institution of the Legislative Assembly, though with full operational and administrative independence in the performance of its duties (Article 183 of the Constitution).

Table 1.1. **Creation of public institutions by decade and by judicial status, Costa Rica**

| Period | Ministries | Autonomous | Semi-autonomous | Subsidiary bodies | Municipalities | State-owned public enterprises | Non-state-owned public enterprises | Total |
|---|---|---|---|---|---|---|---|---|
| Before 1900 | 3 | 2 | 0 | 2 | 32 | 0 | 0 | 39 |
| 1901-10 | 0 | 0 | 0 | 0 | 11 | 0 | 0 | 11 |
| 1911-20 | 0 | 1 | 0 | 0 | 13 | 0 | 0 | 14 |
| 1921-30 | 1 | 3 | 0 | 0 | 3 | 0 | 0 | 7 |
| 1931-40 | 0 | 1 | 0 | 1 | 3 | 0 | 0 | 5 |
| 1941-50 | 0 | 11 | 0 | 1 | 3 | 1 | 6 | 22 |
| 1951-60 | 1 | 5 | 0 | 1 | 0 | 1 | 3 | 11 |
| 1961-70 | 3 | 5 | 1 | 7 | 11 | 0 | 12 | 39 |
| 1971-80 | 4 | 6 | 4 | 16 | 5 | 4 | 9 | 48 |
| 1981-90 | 5 | 2 | 0 | 10 | 0 | 0 | 6 | 23 |
| 1991-2000 | 1 | 3 | 3 | 39 | 0 | 10 | 13 | 69 |
| 2001-10 | 0 | 1 | 0 | 27 | 0 | 4 | 3 | 35 |
| Total | 18 | 40 | 8 | 104 | 81 | 20 | 52 | 323 |

*Source*: Ministry of National Planning and Economic Policy (2015), *Organización del Sector Público en Costa Rica,* Área de Modernización del Estado de MIDEPLAN, Ministry of National Planning and Economic Policy, San José.

## The way forward

Costa Rica has a high level of human development and its governance system has had strong service delivery for more than 50 years. But the socio-economic challenges and the changes in the political system and the administration are putting pressure on the country's governance mechanisms and constrain its aspirations for enhanced and sustainable prosperity for its entire population.

Fiscal and economic pressures are affecting the quality of public services. An increasingly unequal society, remaining levels of poverty and regional disparities affect the citizens' well-being. The government has to deal with economic pressures and make the country more competitive. However, the margin of its fiscal revenue that it can allocate to advance its own policy priorities is small. At the same time, political realities are changing rapidly and contributing to a loss of steering capacity of central government institutions. The Legislative Assembly is often blocked. The Constitutional Chamber has changed the way people interact with the state and a fragmented public sector contributes to an atomisation and dispersion of governance.

But there is an awareness of the challenges ahead and the administration shows a strong commitment to make change happen. The 2015-18 National Development Plan is a testimony of the government's will to move forward towards a more effective, efficient, participatory, open and transparent government that fosters inclusive growth.

Costa Rica is at a turning point: in order to sustain the important historical achievements the country's governance system needs to shift gear and mirror the changing economy and society. Governance reform is needed. As will be discussed in subsequent chapters, this includes, amongst others, moving from processes to results (and ownership thereof), with mutual reinforcement of results-oriented focus both top-down and bottom-up (shifting from compliance tools to management tools) and identifying opportunities to strengthen a shared identity and organisational culture across the public sector.

This OECD Public Governance Review is an opportunity to make a thorough analysis of the current situation of different governance areas and provide input for a reform process that will lead to a more efficient, effective and accountable public administration that focuses on results, delivers better policies and improves the well-being of the population.

## *References*

Alfaro-Redondo, R. and M.A. Seligson (2012), *Cultura política de la democracia en Costa Rica, 2012: La erosión de los pilares de la estabilidad política*, Vanderbilt University, www.vanderbilt.edu/lapop/cr/Costa_Rica_Country_Report_2012_Reduced_W.pdf.

Barker, R.S. (2000), "Judicial review in Costa Rica: Evolution and recent developments", *Southwestern Journal of Law and Trade in the Americas*, Vol. 7, pp. 270-282.

Constitutional Chamber (2014), "Number of cases in the Constitutional Chamber 1989-2012", http://sitios.poder-judicial.go.cr/salaconstitucional/estadisticas.htm.

Gallup World Poll (n.d.), "Gallup World Poll", www.gallup.com/services/170945/world-poll.aspx.

Government of Costa Rica (2014), "Background report", unpublished working paper.

Ministry of Foreign Trade of Costa Rica (2013), "Costa Rica: Evolución del Arancel Promedio, por sector económico, 1995-2003", www.comex.go.cr/estadisticas/aranceles/aranceles%202013/00_Arancel%20promedio%20por%20sector%201995-2013.xlsx.

Ministry of National Planning and Economic Policy (2015), *Organización del Sector Público en Costa Rica*, Área de Modernización del Estado de MIDEPLAN, Ministry of National Planning and Economic Policy, San José.

Ministry of National Planning and Economic Policy (2013), "Organigrama del Sector Público Costarricense", Ministry of National Planning and Economic Policy, San José, http://documentos.mideplan.go.cr/alfresco/d/d/workspace/SpacesStore/57787594-4413-4f0c-9ccd-b6a4e2f6d091/Organigrama%20del%20sector%20p%C3%BAblico%20costarricense%202013.pdf.

OECD (2015), *Revenue Statistics in Latin America and the Caribbean 2015*, OECD Publishing, Paris, http://dx.doi.org/10.1787/rev_lat-2015-en-fr.

OECD (2013), *Government at a Glance 2013*, OECD Publishing, Paris, http://dx.doi.org/10.1787/gov_glance-2013-en.

OECD (2012), "Attracting knowledge-intensive FDI to Costa Rica: Challenges and policy options", *Making Development Happen Series*, No. 1, OECD Publishing, Paris, www.oecd.org/countries/costarica/E-book%20FDI%20to%20Costa%20Rica.pdf.

OECD (2011), *PISA 2009 Results: Students On Line: Digital Technologies and Performance (Volume VI)*, PISA, OECD Publishing, Paris, http://dx.doi.org/10.1787/9789264112995-en.

OECD (2002), *Distributed Public Governance: Agencies, Authorities and other Government Bodies*, OECD Publishing, Paris, http://dx.doi.org/10.1787/9789264177420-en.

OECD/IDB (2014), *Government at a Glance: Latin America and the Caribbean 2014: Towards Innovative Public Financial Management*, OECD Publishing, Paris, http://dx.doi.org/10.1787/9789264209480-en.

Presidential Commission on Democratic Governance (2013), "Propuestas para fortalecer la funcionalidad y calidad de la democracia costarricense", Informe final, Presidential Commission on Democratic Governance, www.eap.ucr.ac.cr/index.php/eap-apps/descarga-de-archivos/category/44-otros?download=296:informe-de-notables.

Programa Estado de la Nación (2014), *Informe Estado de la Nación*, CONARE (National Council of Rectors), San José, www.estadonacion.or.cr/20.

Programa Estado de la Nación (2013), *Informe Estado de la Nación*, CONARE (National Council of Rectors), San José, www.estadonacion.or.cr/estado-nacion/nacion-informes-anteriores/informes-2001-2011/xix-informe-2013.

Republic of Costa Rica (1949), *Constitución Política de la Rèpublica de Costa Rica*, www.constitution.org/cons/costaric.htm.

Transparency International (2014), "Corruption by country/territory – Costa Rica", Transparency International, www.transparency.org/country#CRI.

UNDP (2014), *La Equidad en Costa Rica: Incidencia de la Política Social y la Política Fiscal*, United Nations Development Programme, www.cr.undp.org/content/dam/costa_rica/docs/undp_cr_equidad_2014.pdf.

UNDP (2013), *Human Development Report 2013: The Rise of the South: Human Progress in a Diverse World*, United Nations Development Programme, New York, http://hdr.undp.org/sites/default/files/reports/14/hdr2013_en_complete.pdf.

UNICEF (2013), "At a glance: Costa Rica", www.unicef.org/infobycountry/costarica_statistics.html.

Wise, M.B. (2010), "Judicial review and its politicization in Central America: Guatemala, Costa Rica, and constitutional limits on presidential candidates", *Santa Clara Journal of International Law*, Vol. 7, Issue 2, Article 4, http://digitalcommons.law.scu.edu/scujil/vol7/iss2/4.

World Bank (2014a), *Costa Rica Overview*, www.worldbank.org/en/country/costarica/overview.

World Bank (2014b), *Doing Business 2015: Going Beyond Efficiency*, 12th edition, International Bank for Reconstruction and Development/The World Bank, Washington, DC, www.doingbusiness.org/reports/global-reports/doing-business-2015.

World Economic Forum (2013), *The Global Competitiveness Report 2013-2014: Full Data Edition*, World Economic Forum, Geneva, www3.weforum.org/docs/WEF_GlobalCompetitivenessReport_2013-14.pdf.

# *Chapter 2.*

# Enhancing centre of government co-ordination capacity in Costa Rica

*This chapter analyses the role of the centre of government (CoG) in Costa Rica. The chapter elaborates upon OECD tendencies in this area, which underline a shift from a primary administrative support function for the CoG to a position as strategic player with important responsibilities to foster vision, leadership and innovation across the public sector. Country-specific challenges are identified for Costa Rica and these include the high-level of political and public sector fragmentation, as well as capacity constraints at both the technical and strategic level. The chapter formulates recommendations to strengthen the CoG, which include targeted capacity building, a revised model of co-ordinating the institutionally decentralised sector and the introduction of multi-stakeholder follow-up mechanisms for key policy areas.*

## The centre of government as strategic player

### *From administrative support to policy co-ordination*

The centre of government (CoG) is the body or group of bodies that provides direct support and advice to the head of government and the Council of Ministers. The CoG is known under different labels in different countries, such as the Chancellery, Cabinet Office, Office of the President, *Presidencia*, etc. From its traditional role of serving the executive from an administrative perspective, the CoG is now playing a more active role in policy development and co-ordination across OECD Members. The centre in many countries now provides services that range from strategic planning to real-time policy advice and intelligence, and from leading major cross-departmental policy initiatives to monitoring progress and outcomes (OECD, 2014b).

The extended definition of the CoG does not only refer to the Presidency or its equivalent, but also comprises key strategic partners, such as the Ministry of Finance (where policy priorities are matched with resources) or a Ministry of Planning (with an important role in designing policy priorities across the administration and how these contribute to an overall strategic plan). As such, and depending on the particular situation of a country in terms of its institutional constellation, several actors can play an important role in CoG co-ordination. Additionally, central agencies responsible for a coherent human resources (HR) policy, e-government policy, regulatory policy, etc. across different departments also contribute to a reinforced cross-governmental co-ordination.

Generally speaking – i.e. cross-presidential, parliamentary and other systems – the three key roles of the centre are: 1) supporting quality decision making by the head of government; 2) policy co-ordination across government; and 3) monitoring of the implementation of government policy. With its ambition to mobilise and influence (very often) larger, budget-holding departments across government, the CoG's success depends not only on formal powers or structures but also, to a large extent, on its capacity to lead and motivate (Figure 2.1 gives an overview of the primary focus of CoG institutions across OECD Members based on the OECD Survey of Centres of Government).

Figure 2.1. **Focus of the centre of government: Primary focus of centre of government institutions across OECD Members**

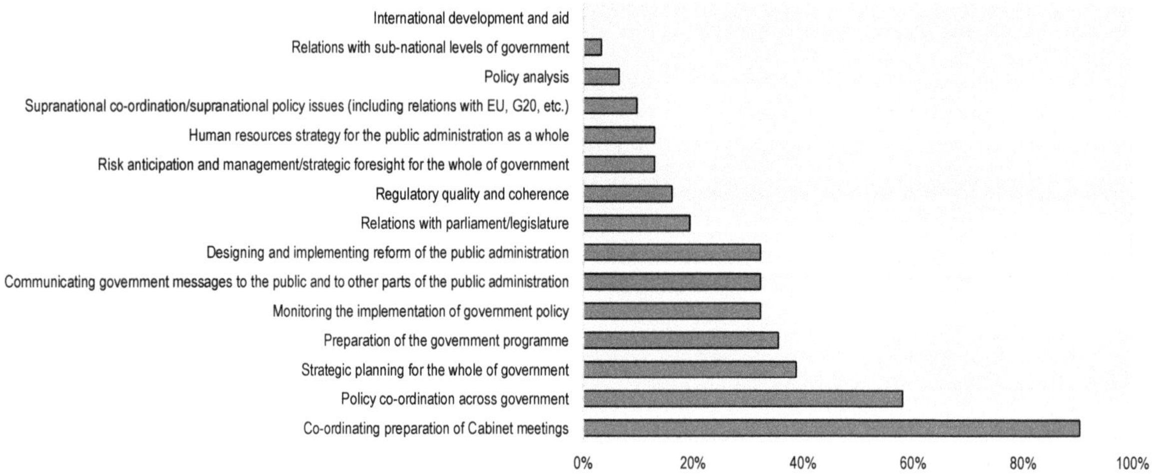


*Source:* OECD (2014b), "Centre stage: Driving better policies from the centre of government", GOV/PGC/MPM(2014)3/FINAL, OECD, Paris, www.oecd.org/gov/Centre-Stage-Report.pdf.

The OECD Survey of Centres of Government also shows that a majority of countries (59%) confirm that the number of cross-ministerial policy initiatives has increased over the past few years (2008-12), and almost all respondents reported that leading policy co-ordination has now become one of the priority tasks of the centre (OECD, 2014b). The centre can lead such cross-ministerial co-ordination by: 1) integrating cross-disciplinary perspectives (including its own perspective – the centre is not "policy neutral") into policy advice for the head of government and/or Cabinet; 2) leading policy co-ordination via both traditional committee architectures and more innovative and informal channels; 3) facilitating resource sharing through a closer partnership with ministries of finance; and 4) supporting experimentation and testing of new delivery systems, many of which are based on shared service models.

Leading strategic initiatives is delicate, particularly in countries in which authority is highly decentralised. It is essential to offer both short- and long-term gains to senior public officials as incentives to co-operate in complex initiatives that involve risk-, resource- and accountability sharing. For example, the long-term gains of achieving a culture change among senior civil servants so that they are used to working with each other should be matched with some shorter term "rewards" for changing their behaviour and investing time in new practices.

### *Centre of government anno 2014: Vision, leadership and innovation*

The OECD's work on centres of government explores how governments can adapt the institutions at the centre in order to play an expanded and more outward-looking role. With declining trust figures across countries in the aftermath of the crisis, the CoG's leadership and innovative decision-making capacity is more decisive than ever before to ensure that government has a clear vision for a country's future, is capable of engaging in a dialogue with the administration and citizens on this vision, and manages to deliver so as to foster sustainable long-term growth and well-being (OECD, 2013a).

Box 2.1 provides a more detailed overview of how vision, leadership and innovation are central to the CoG's daily business these days. Across these three areas of vision, leadership and innovation, the capacity of bridging the (potential) gap between political staff (ministries, state secretaries, political advisors and senior civil servants in certain cases) and the civil service is one of the challenges of incoming governments. To that end, it is noteworthy that some countries specifically invest in training for new political staff (OECD, 2014a). Examples include, for instance Iceland, where the Government Office runs formal training programmes for new ministers, or the United States, where the Office of Management and Budget runs training led by former political appointees.

In addition to the CoG's responsibility to display vision, leadership and innovation capacity, previous OECD Public Governance Reviews (OECD, 2014c) have shown that an effective CoG is also critical for:

- Accountability. The CoG is the steward for strategic vision. It is accountable for overall results and oversight of the delegated responsibilities. It is important, however, to avoid overly rigid "command and control" structures and micro-management, but instead, to work towards a system where the CoG can exert effective oversight and clarify lines of accountability. Line ministries need to exercise leadership for the actions and policies for which they are responsible, within the overall framework of a shared collective commitment.

### Box 2.1. Centre of government – observations and trends in 2014: Vision, leadership and innovation

The success of a government rests on its ability to define a vision for the country that reflects an electoral mandate and that is typically designed to increase well-being, prosperity and international competitiveness. In the years following the economic crisis, concern with budgets dominated in most countries, crowding out any other vision. However, those days appear to be over, and governments are seeking to be more forward-looking and strategic. Most OECD Members have some sort of vision document these days. This vision has different, interlinked dimensions, including a long-term vision for the nation, usually going beyond growth objectives to embrace well-being and sustainability goals, and a vision for what the government of the day wants to achieve.

The government no longer has a monopoly on defining the vision. While efforts to gather citizens' views could risk raising expectations that cannot be fulfilled, such bottom-up visions can help validate and legitimise government policy. Vision depends on two crucial factors that were mentioned repeatedly in the debate: trust and communication. If citizens do not trust the government, they will not trust its vision. Taking steps to strengthen trust in government more generally will help to ensure greater buy-in on more strategic goals. Communication and ownership are also important. If the vision has a strong narrative, connects to citizens' lives and is well communicated, then it can help generate support for difficult reforms. A particular problem faced by policy makers is that the reform process and its translation into real benefits for citizens are often too slow, undermining confidence and enthusiasm for longer term visions.

Leadership is crucial to drive policies that contribute to a strategic vision. In a complex and challenging policy environment, characterised by low levels of trust in government, leadership is an essential attribute of effective government. Room for manoeuvre of governments has probably diminished at both the national level, because of budgetary pressure, and at the international level, because of globalisation. Nevertheless, the centre guides in terms of substance and helps departments understand how to align policies with broader objectives. And the centre also has a role to play in leading by example, promoting efficiency and good policy management by departments. A key issue is to ensure that the civil service and the political staff do not become disconnected, working as separate entities at the centre.

Many centres of government actively promote innovation in their public services, with an emphasis on encouraging a culture of innovation in public services and providing a stable frame for policy innovation and creativity. The centre can provide an impetus – particularly when it partners with specialist agencies that can identify talented people, good ideas and "roll-out" techniques. Some countries have successfully used innovation focal points or dedicated units to drive public sector innovation; at the same time, being the innovation leader requires appropriate financial and human resources.

*Source:* OECD (2014a), "Vision, leadership, innovation: Driving public policy performance", 33rd Meeting of Senior Officials from Centres of Government, OECD, Paris, www.oecd.org/gov/summary.pdf.

- Strategic planning, policy coherence and collective commitment. The CoG needs the capacity to give the strategic vision specific shape, to secure its coherence and to make it operational. A starting point is likely to be the government programme or equivalent, giving effect to the political manifesto of the party or parties in power. Making the strategic vision operational is key, otherwise the vision is a "dead letter". The doctrine of collective responsibility is crucial to bind line ministries as well as the CoG to a course of action. Collective commitment is also, crucially, built, developed, discussed and agreed by the whole range of actors that are engaged in public policy making, implementation and service delivery.

- Communication. The CoG needs the capacity to communicate the strategic vision, how it is being taken forward and its implementation. Transparency and openness help to promote a shared sense of purpose, for stakeholders outside as well as inside the government. Clarity of communication within the administration is important so that, for example, decentralised institutions can understand the vision and share in its construction and so that all parts of the public sector understand their role, responsibility and accountability for results.

Given its comprehensive set of responsibilities, the CoG also requires sustainability across political cycles (OECD, 2014c). CoG institutions are best constructed, as far as possible, to withstand the vagaries of the political cycle and to be sustainable over the time that it takes to implement long-term strategies. Stability of core functions and structures will raise confidence that the strategic vision is taken seriously and that the country will have the institutional capacity, over time, to carry out the vision. To carry out its strategic role effectively, the CoG needs to foster collective commitment and partner with the agencies that provide services on its behalf (Box 2.2) and clearly communicate its strategic vision (Box 2.3).

## Centre of government in Costa Rica: The institutional set-up

The CoG operates in support of the President of the Republic and the Council of Ministers. The President of the Republic acts as head of state and head of government and, together with the appropriate Cabinet minister, has functions including the ability (Article 140 of the Constitution) to appoint and remove employees who hold "positions of trust"; the initiative to enact laws and the right of veto; the collection and expenditure of the national revenues; the oversight of the proper operation of administrative services and agencies, among others. The Council of Ministers is chaired by the President of the Republic and composed of the ministers, according to Article 147 of the Constitution of 1949 and Law 6227 of 1978. Its main functions include advising the President, dealing with the issues delegated by him/her and nominating ambassadors and the heads of autonomous institutions. In practice, the Council of Ministers serves the purpose of a co-ordination body, where the President can monitor progress on strategic issues. The President has the right to revise the decision of the Council.

The CoG capacity (in the broad sense) is distributed across the following institutions:[1]

- The Ministry of the Presidency: created by Article 23 of the Public Administration General Act of Law 6227. As defined in the Budget of the Republic Act 2015, the Ministry of the Presidency is responsible for exercising political and technical guidance to the President in its decision making, which allows greater welfare of the population through communication and co-ordination. Traditionally, the ministry has been in charge of co-ordination between the Presidency and the legislature, as well as with other entities.
- The Ministry of National Planning and Economic Policy (*Ministerio de Planificación Nacional y Política Económica*, MIDEPLAN): its primary duties include the preparation of the National Development Plan (NDP); the verification that public investment projects across government entities are aligned with priorities set forth in the NDP; approval of investment projects of public agencies when such projects are externally financed or government approval is required; amongst others (Articles 9, 10 and 11, National Planning Act of Law 5525 of 1974). Through these functions, the ministry gives technical and political advice to the Presidency of the Republic and other public institutions, while it

formulates, co-ordinates, monitors and evaluates the strategies and priorities of the government.

- Ministry of Finance (*Ministerio de Hacienda*) – co-ordinates the budgetary cycle for the central government budget (i.e. ministries and their subsidiary bodies). The Ministry of Finance has competences regarding central government budget, public accounting, management of state property, management of the internal and external debt, public procurement, among others. In addition, responsibilities include its contribution to the stability and economic growth for social development through the collection, management, allocation, accountability and proper use of financial resources.

Box 2.2. **Fostering collective commitment: The cases of the United Kingdom and New Zealand**

To foster collective commitment between government departments, on the one hand, and agencies providing public services on behalf of the government, on the other, the following factors proved essential in the UK experience:

- clarity of accountabilities, roles and responsibilities
- strategic alignment
- financial and performance management
- communications and engagement
- relationship management based on mutual trust and respect and a real understanding of each other's objectives.

In New Zealand's Crown entity system, efforts to foster collective commitment include three actors: ministers, entities and monitoring departments. To work together effectively, a framework sets out the roles, responsibilities and expectations for all three parties. The expectations are aligned horizontally so that each of the three parties is aware of what is expected of the other parties. Statutory Crown entities operate with three sets of expectations:

- The Enduring Letter of Expectations from the Ministers of Finance and State Services.
- Ministerial expectations, which inform entities' strategic direction over the next four years (set out in their statements of intent) and priorities for the coming year (set out in their statements of performance expectations).
- Operating expectations, which guide engagement between the statutory entity, its responsible minister and the monitoring department. These are intended to help the parties achieve trusting, productive relationships.

The following four principles guide the expectations' framework:

- clear roles and responsibilities
- strategic alignment
- efficient and effective monitoring
- trusted engagement.

*Sources:* Ministry for Culture and Heritage of New Zealand (2014), *Statutory Crown Entities – It Takes Three: Operating Expectations Framework*, Crown Copyright, www.ssc.govt.nz/sites/all/files/it-takes-three-operating-expectations-framework.pdf; Rutter, J. et al. (2012), "It takes two: How to create effective relationships between government and arm's-length bodies", Institute for Government, London, www.instituteforgovernment.org.uk/sites/default/files/publications/it_takes_two_final_0.pdf.

**Box 2.3. Communication of a country's strategic vision and its implementation: The case of Colombia**

Colombia has developed and refined a comprehensive system of information to monitor and evaluate the extent to which the country is reaching its main goals. This system, inspired by international experiences such as the Delivery Unit in the United Kingdom and the White House Dashboards, has enabled Colombia to discuss priorities and identify major challenges. Through it, Colombia has integrated all of the information from the different entities and sectors, with diverse indicators, clear guidelines and targets. Through a complete set of indicators, the country managed to develop user-friendly dashboards and traffic lights to display the information. In addition, National Development Plan Perception Surveys are conducted periodically so as to compare public perception and government results. The results of the polls are public and are found on the SISDEVAL (Sistema Nacional de Evaluaciones) website. Surveys measure perception of the way the government is achieving the goals set.

*Source:* OECD (2013b), *Colombia: Implementing Good Governance*, OECD Public Governance Reviews, OECD Publishing, Paris, http://dx.doi.org/10.1787/9789264202177-en.

- Budgetary Authority: initially created in 1979 by decree. The current legislation is provided by Law No. 8131 on Financial Administration of the Republic. The law defines the Budgetary Authority as a collegiate body in charge of advising the President on budgetary policy. According to Article 23 of the law, the Budgetary Authority proposes the general and specific budgetary guidelines for the following year for the central government, including its decentralised bodies and the state-owned enterprises. The final approval of such binding guidelines is done by the President, after its presentation in the Council of Ministers. The Budgetary Authority has three members: the Minister of Finance (or vice minister), as chair, the Minister of Planning (or vice minister), a minister (or vice minister) nominated by the President of the Republic. In addition, the Budgetary Authority has an Executive Directorate and a Technical Secretariat.

Next to these institutions, the following (*ad hoc*) instruments contribute to the CoG's co-ordination capacity:

- Costa Rica 2030, National Development Goals: published in 2013 by MIDEPLAN with the support of the UNDP, complementary to the four-year National Development Plan. The report presents a long-term view for the country, was built upon a public consultation process and has a monitoring and evaluation framework incorporated. There is no explicit link with a (medium-term) budgeting process or with the National Development Plan. The government is currently launching a council of experts from academia, the private sector, the public sector and the organised civil society to assure evaluation of these National Development Goals. The council, along with MIDEPLAN, will also choose the methodology and four key topics that will be addressed in a new long-term strategy, in line with the National Planning System's legal framework, i.e. displaying (minimally) a 20-year perspective.
- National Development Plan (NDP): on 17 November 2014, a new NDP for 2015-18 was presented, following the change of government of Costa Rica. The elaboration of the new NDP was driven by three main guidelines: 1) strategic orientation, with strong focus on performance management, including the national, sectorial and regional dimensions; 2) public consultation and active

participation of the various actors responsible for the implementation of the plan, to ensure its compliance; 3) assure that the monitoring and evaluation provides information not only on the achieved goals but also on the products, effects and impacts achieved in social welfare. MIDEPLAN co-ordinated the drafting process with the institutions, involving approximately 100 public bodies and entities, and drafted regional and sectorial proposals while taking into account the national priorities. The elaboration of the NDP is characterised by a prospective vision, a mid- and long-term approach, in order to develop the country and eradicate poverty, with increased equality and environmental sustainability. The time horizon therefore now surpasses the four-year mandate of the government, reinforcing the strategic vision to formulate national policies. Nevertheless, as mentioned previously, no explicit link is made with the 2030 National Development Goals. The three basic pillars of the new administration for the definition of policy goals and targets are: 1) promote economic growth and quality employment; 2) fight poverty and inequality; and 3) open government, transparency, efficiency and fight against corruption. The principles guiding the new model of development contained in the NDP 2015-18 are: promote citizen participation through dialogue roundtables; solidarity, considering the rights of the vulnerable population and local governments; environmental sustainability and risk management; equity and equality; responsibility and improved management of public investment projects; ethics, accountability; open government, transparency in public service, prevention and control of corruption; universal accessibility; the *Tejiendo Desarrollo* project (oriented towards territorial development) and employment. The new NDP considers it essential to promote citizen participation and foster transparency, in order to enable society to perform the function of control and surveillance of public actions. Therefore, the NDP envisages generating mechanisms, initiatives and instruments of citizen participation in decision making on public policy.

- National Planning System (NPS): regulated by Law 5525 of 1974, the National Planning System is the key mechanism for the monitoring and evaluation of public policies, plans, programmes, projects and strategic actions of the government in a systematic, public, independent and participative way. The general objective of the NPS is to enhance the sustainable development of the country through the exercise of planning, with a focus on intensifying growth production and productivity, promoting a better income distribution and social services, and promoting increasing citizen participation. The NPS' responsibilities cover analytical work on socio-economic themes, development of policy proposals for economic and social development, participation in the preparation of and adopting the National Development Policy, co-ordination of the latter and the evaluation of obtained results. The General Regulations of the NPS enumerate a set of principles: adaptability, co-ordination, effectiveness, equity, impartiality, integration, legality, opportunity, participation, reasonability, simplicity, transparency, universality and binding nature. The regulations also refer to the different planning instruments existing in Costa Rica. Finally, they establish that the institutions comprising the NPS shall develop permanent actions to effectively incorporate social and productive sectors, and citizens in general, in the formulation of planning instruments. MIDEPLAN is the head of the NPS, which further comprises sectorial councils, sectorial secretariats, rector ministers and planning offices in each institution.

- Sector planning and co-ordination (Executive Decree 38536): defines the organisation of the sector co-ordination (currently 16 sectors in total). Each sector comprises central and decentralised institutions. The sector co-ordination responsibility lies with the head of the central government institution, not the institution itself. The sector co-ordinator can count on the technical support of a secretariat. Only a few sectors have established formal secretariats that are distinct from the ministerial structure. The co-ordinator appoints a technical liaison who co-ordinates with MIDEPLAN the processes and procedures relating to the preparation of the NDP. Likewise, the liaison is in charge of co-ordinating with other institutions in the same sector.
- Interministerial Commission Planning-Hacienda (set up in 2011 by Executive Decree No. 36901): composed of representatives of MIDEPLAN and of the Ministry of Finance. The purpose of the commission is to issue and standardise technical and methodological guidelines for programming, monitoring and evaluating budget execution at its different levels (strategic, sectorial and institutional), with the view of ensuring simplification of procedures, guiding the public sector during the planning-budgeting cycle. The most important accomplishments of the commission since its creation include promoting a better understanding of the differences and similarities between the ministries' planning and budgeting mechanisms; harmonisation of a framework of strategic concepts that allow a link between planning for results and budgeting for results; incorporation of gender and inclusiveness guidelines in the planning-budgeting cycle; first attempts to elaborate a medium-term expenditure framework (MTEF) for 2013-18. The remaining challenges of the commission included in its work plan until the end of 2015 are the continuous improvement of methodological guidelines, to become clearer, unique, inclusive and outcome-oriented; the design of methodologies for the calculation of the cost of public goods and services, starting with pilot cases; awareness raising among civil servants of the importance of an MTEF; incorporation of risk management criteria. The development of a co-ordinated instrument for planning and budgeting in public sector institutions has been identified as a top priority of the commission.
- Presidential councils: regulated by decree, attached to the President of the Republic, composed of ministers (or their representatives) and other public institutions. Their functions include advising, orientation and co-ordination of public policies, as well as planning and design objectives, goals, actions, indicators and control mechanisms. Additionally, they can take into account the stakeholders' views. To this end, the President can nominate leaders or intellectuals as advising bodies on specific topics. To ensure adequate feedback, representatives of the private sector, academics or civil society leaders can be involved. Ministerial councils were initially created in 2010 (Executive Decree 36024), including the establishment of the Presidential Council on Competitiveness and Innovation and the Presidential Council on Social and Family Well-being in 2011 (Executive Decree 36467). In 2014, Executive Decree 38662 further revised the structure and functioning of the Presidential Council on Competiveness and Innovation.
- Better Regulation Commission: an advisory body attached to the Ministry of Economy, Industry and Trade, set up in 1995 by Law 7472 of Competition and Consumer Effective Protection. Its main functions are to co-ordinate and lead the regulatory initiatives; analyse specific proposals from public institutions or

citizens for bureaucratic and regulatory simplification and reduction of administrative burdens; and recommend the implementation of corrective actions in order to increase efficiency on specific regulations. The commission is chaired by the Minister of Economy, Industry and Trade, and is also composed of high-level representatives of the Ministries of Health, Environment and Energy, Agriculture, as well as the President of the Competency Commission, and a representative of the several sectorial chambers. For 2015, the President announced that 195 procedures (i.e. 3 procedures per institution involved) should be simplified by the end of October 2015, for which the Ministry of Economy, Industry and Trade will assure monitoring through reporting to the President every 4 months.

- Thematic cross-government co-ordination with legal basis: such as Law 9137 on the initiative to integrate efforts to reduce poverty into one centralised system comprising all beneficiaries of relevant programmes and institutions ("National System of Information and Single Registry of State Beneficiaries"). In that context, an entity attached to the Mixed Institute of Social Aid was created in 2013 to constitute an updated country-wide database with information about people requesting services, assistance, subsidies and economic aid for those in poverty or vulnerable situations, eliminate duplicated actions of social protection to the families in need of assistance, determination of a single methodology to measure poverty levels. For that purpose, the entity developed a database, constituted an inter-institutional network, ensured co-ordination of different institutions working on poverty eradication, and monitored and evaluated the effectiveness of related programmes. Finally, a council was created to facilitate compliance with the objective, composed of senior civil servants of the Mixed Institute of Social Aid, MIDEPLAN and the Ministries of Education, Health, Housing, Employment and Social Security, *inter alia.*

## Costa Rica's centre of government challenges

As for most OECD Members, Costa Rica faces the "new" CoG challenges such as the push for a longer term strategic vision, including a clear strategy on how to incorporate citizens' input in this process. The development – and implementation – of the new NDP is a critical process for the country in this respect.

In addition, Costa Rica grapples with some country-specific CoG co-ordination challenges, including:

- political fragmentation, hampering overall policy-making capacity, and hence, putting pressure on the strategic leverage of the CoG
- public sector fragmentation, in particular because of the operating principles (in terms of autonomy and steering) of the institutionally decentralised sector
- capacity constraints at both technical and strategic level across CoG actors, fostered by substantial turnover of staff that accompanies a change of government and reflecting a certain degree of path dependency in policy-making practices (e.g. more focus on policy planning than the analysis of strategic policy performance).

The challenge of ensuring national level co-ordination in a setting characterised by public sector fragmentation due to the creation of agencies and decentralisation, is not unique to Costa Rica alone. Box 2.4 synthesises lessons learnt and practical recommendations following a research programme on the creation and operation of public sector agencies in 30 countries.

### Box 2.4. Agencies and public sector fragmentation: Lessons and recommendations from 30 countries

**Lessons learnt:**

- Extensive agencification in systems with weak co-ordination capacity may endanger system effectiveness.
- Rationalisation of agencies is not an absolute guarantee for better performance or more co-ordination; the approach and criteria for the rationalisation matter.
- The choice of agencies as an organisational form for public tasks happens in many countries in a rather *ad hoc* or unsystematic way.
- The overall autonomy of an agency is actually a product of balancing managerial, policy, financial and legal autonomy. There are, however, no straightforward relationships between these different kinds of autonomy (legal, financial, managerial and policy autonomy).
- While the level of perceived managerial autonomy of agencies differs considerably between countries and within countries, the level of policy autonomy of agencies in many countries seems to be rather substantial.
- Steering and control of agencies requires new skills and competencies of parent ministries and other principals, which fit with a more horizontal, contractual relationship.
- Steering agencies at arm's length requires the development of new instruments and organisational arrangements, which fit with a more horizontal relationship.

**Recommendations:**

- Consider elements like the creation, autonomy, control and management, and co-ordination of agencies, in an integrated way.
- Invest in better co-ordination by improving the connection between policy and implementation, and between financial and performance information. Create incentives and cross-cutting targets for collaboration among agencies and between agencies and other organisations.
- Create more transparency about agency models and types, for example by setting up a register of agencies, as well as criteria and checklists for agencification decisions. Limit institutional variety and the number of agency types to a level that is manageable and transparent, while leaving sufficient scope for context-specific design. Link agency types and governance more to the tasks and functions of agencies where possible.
- Consider more carefully the combination of different kinds of autonomy which are given to a specific agency (formal/legal, managerial autonomy with regards to personnel and financial management, policy autonomy, financial autonomy).
- Review periodically the compatibility of formal regulations with actual practice in order to better align these, while avoiding that such adaptations of the legal framework lead to more procedures and regulations, hampering flexibility.

Box 2.4. **Agencies and public sector fragmentation: Lessons and recommendations from 30 countries** (*cont.*)

- Involve the implementation expertise of agencies in the policy development process, without hollowing out the role of parent ministries as main initiator, co-ordinator and manager of the policy development process.
- Invest in new models and instruments for steering agencies at arm's length, for example performance dialogue, trust and account management. Consider performance contracts primarily as instruments to improve communication, exchange, negotiation and mutual learning between parent ministries and agencies, instead of contracts in a legal sense with a focus on harsh sanctions.
- Strike a balance between autonomy (letting go) and control (keeping in touch) in building and maintaining good relationships with agencies. Consider a risk-based and dynamic approach to control agencies in order to reduce the control burdens for parent ministries and agencies alike.
- A relationship is mutual; make sure that agencies are involved in (policy and management) decisions that concern them.
- Pay sufficient attention in developing parliamentary and extra-parliamentary instruments (like ombudsmen, public reporting) to hold agencies accountable. Horizontal accountability instruments towards peers and customers is important in this regard.

*Source:* Verhoest, K. et al. (2011), "Governing public agencies in the 21st century: International lessons and policy recommendations", COST Office, KU Leuven, Public Management Institute, Leuven, Belgium, http://soc.kuleuven.be/io/cost/act/pdf/20110527_Brussels/COST_policy_brochure_for%20conference.pdf.

Box 2.5 provides an insightful overview of the co-ordination opportunities and challenges a key CoG actor in Costa Rica, MIDEPLAN, is currently facing to follow-up the NDP implementation in a context of a fragmented public sector, and it reflects the interplay of the three aforementioned challenges (political fragmentation, public sector fragmentation and capacity constraints).

## *Coping with public sector fragmentation*

As discussed in Chapter 1, Costa Rica faces substantial fragmentation of the public sector. Institutionally decentralised public entities and subsidiary bodies of central government ministries are one of the key features of the country's governance system. Formally, and regardless of the variance of the purpose, nature, legal framework and degree of independence (financially and administratively) of the institutionally decentralised entities, the Financial Administration and Public Budgets Act and the National Planning Act establish that the budget and investment projects of all decentralised institutions must be aligned with the National Development Plan (Article 4, Financial Administration and Public Budgets Act, Law 8131 of 2001; and Article 9, National Planning Act, Law 5525 of 1974).

Whereas most of the initial entities of the institutionally decentralised sector were created in the 1940s as autonomous institutions with a mandate of policy making as well as service delivery such as health, energy and education, a more recent wave of newly created public institutions primarily consists of subsidiary bodies, representing "policy implementation shortcuts" to attain greater administrative and budgetary flexibility

(Government of Costa Rica, 2014). Whereas this creates flexibility, it impacts on the CoG co-ordination capacity subsequently, as was repeatedly flagged by different stakeholders.

Box 2.5. **Centre of government co-ordination constraints and opportunities: The NDP**

A brainstorming session with MIDEPLAN on its current co-ordination capacity (i.e. including the institutionally decentralised sector) for the NDP provided an insightful overview of the co-ordination opportunities and challenges the institution is facing:

- importance of distinguishing between dimensions of steering, co-ordination and accountability, i.e. to understand how these differ, complement each other, can be used strategically, and how these dimensions shape the interaction between vertical and horizontal actors
- board composition of the institutionally decentralised sector (e.g. added value of having the rector for sector co-ordination as board member for strategic autonomous entities), and impact of board nomination cycle (i.e. not necessarily coinciding with political cycle)
- potential added value of "soft" instruments like a code of conduct for both the institutionally decentralised entities and their boards to foster principles of transparency and accountability, commitment to NDP goals, etc.
- importance of the capacity and credibility of actors responsible for horizontal co-ordination
- the added value (and limitations) of individual agencies' performance goals in the new NDP
- the potential of performance reporting as opposed to compliance reporting (combined with reduction of the reporting burden)
- the impact of perceived sector political priority, leadership and personal relationships
- the impact of the constitutionally and legally binding budgetary allocations
- the role of ultimate decision-making power of the President (i.e. removal of head of autonomous institution)
- the potential to increase accountability of the institutionally decentralised sector towards citizens.

### *Co-ordination capacity, roles and responsibilities*

In terms of CoG capacity, Alessandro, Lafuente and Santiso (2013) identify eight types of CoG units which reflect CoG core competences and can be arranged in different configurations:

1. chief executive's direct support unit: offices that provide direct personal support to the President or the Prime Minister, including political and logistical assistance and managing both logistics and political affairs (e.g. White House Office in the United States, Prime Minister's Office in the United Kingdom)
2. strategy units: devoted to the task of preparing the government's main strategic initiatives (e.g. Prime Minister's Strategy Unit in the 2002-10 UK Cabinet Office)
3. policy co-ordination units: a co-ordinating function, either by supporting and facilitating environments for policy co-ordination to occur (e.g. preparing Cabinet

meetings or interministerial committees), or by being directly involved in the contents of policy

4. performance monitoring units: focused on measuring the results that the policies are producing through a limited number of strategic, high-level indicators (e.g. the United Kingdom's Prime Minister's Delivery Unit, or the *Unidad Presidencial de Gestión de Cumplimiento* in Chile)
5. press, communications and speechwriting unit: in charge of co-ordinating the government's communications, ensuring a coherent message across the different ministries and agencies
6. policy advice units and individual advisors: in order to diversify their sources of information, chief executives sometimes have experts on their staff in areas that are the responsibility of line ministries (e.g. Council of Economic Advisers in the United States)
7. legal counsel unit: reviews the legality of the proposals sent by the departments to the chief executive
8. internal management unit: carrying out administrative duties needed for the CoG to properly function.

Referring back to the section on the main CoG actors and instruments (i.e. including competencies of the Presidency, MIDEPLAN and presidential councils), it shows that a substantial part of the strategy, policy co-ordination, performance monitoring and policy advice functions is rather located at MIDEPLAN, complemented with a relatively important role for (a limited number of) presidential councils. However, there is a substantial risk that – because of the scope of its duties, as well as its institutional embeddedness – MIDEPLAN is fully occupied with the technical and operational responsibility of policy co-ordination and performance monitoring, which does not necessarily have the same impact and leverage it would have if these responsibilities (at a strategic, rather than operational level) were embedded in a unit close to the President. Box 2.6 provides some examples of the set-up of strategic performance units in other countries.

Based on its organisational chart, the Presidency primarily focuses on its role of presidential management (including legal aspects), support services, information and communication, and on being the Secretariat for the Council of Ministers. However, the Budget of the Republic Act 2015 states that the Ministry of Presidency "is responsible for exercising political and technical guidance to President in its decision making, which allows greater welfare of the population through communication and co-ordination".[2] Referring to the Presidency's current organisational chart, this responsibility might benefit from a more explicit visibility in the organisational chart and possibly be strengthened in terms of actual capacity. Box 2.7 shows an example of areas in which the Presidency could provide guidance with respect to the preparation of high-level government meetings and also indicates to what extent this is the case in other OECD Members.

Next to a clear definition of CoG actors' responsibilities, the stability of the CoG is important in order to develop a strong CoG co-ordination capacity throughout time and to establish a solid reputation as an institutional actor. In this respect, it is instrumental to consider the changes in MIDEPLAN's mandate and position throughout time. Over time, there have been shifts in the institutional anchorage (from an office within the Presidency to a separate ministry in the 1980s) as well as very substantial changes in the scope of its mandate (e.g. diminishing involvement in the budgetary process in the 1980s and 1990s, active involvement in state reform processes in the 1980s and 1990s, expanding role in the interaction with the municipalities after 2000, reactivation of its role in public investment planning in the 2000s, recent strengthening of its role in evaluation, etc.). Whereas some evolution in the scope of mandate is natural, aspects of appropriate capacity and suitable strategic anchorage to successfully fulfil these different tasks should be considered carefully, so as not to jeopardise the CoG's co-ordination capacity for each of these important cross-government responsibilities. A certain level of stability is indeed needed for accumulating knowledge and experience, as it helps to build relationships of authority and control within and across institutions.

Box 2.6. **Implementation units in Australia, the United Kingdom and Malaysia**

Countries such as Australia, the United Kingdom and Malaysia have established implementation units within their central agencies at different times to monitor policy and programme implementation. These units may have the role of pre-implementation review of proposed programmes to determine their readiness for implementation, or may have a monitoring role to ensure effective implementation. These implementation units use a combination of hard levers (e.g. formal implementation analysis) as well as a variety of soft levers, such as training and the exchange of best practices, to improve implementation performance.

The Prime Minister's Delivery Unit in the **United Kingdom** under Prime Minster Blair, used quantitative indicators to measure how the departments were performing on the Prime Minister's top priorities and could intervene with a targeted action in case adjustments were required. The role of the Prime Minister's Delivery Unit was as follows: the Prime Minister's Delivery Unit aims to help to deliver better and more efficient public services by monitoring and reporting on delivery of the Prime Minister's top delivery and reform priorities; identifying the key barriers to improvement and the action needed to strengthen delivery; strengthening departments' capacity to deliver, through capability reviews and sharing knowledge about best practice in delivery; and supporting the development of high-quality public service agreement targets that will effectively incentivise improvements in public services (UK Cabinet Office, 2006).

The Cabinet Implementation Unit in **Australia**, established in 2003 in the Department of Prime Minister and Cabinet, aims to ensure a rigorous follow-up on the implementation of policies: "The Cabinet Implementation Unit provides support and advice to the Prime Minister on the development, implementation and delivery of the government's strategic priorities. This includes the preparation of regular reports to the Prime Minister on the progress with key policy initiatives. It also includes working collaboratively with departments and agencies to improve the planning, implementation and delivery of key government priorities" (Australian Government, 2012). The Cabinet Implementation Unit conducts regular, short implementation planning "workouts" to provide agencies with practical information to help improve implementation planning. The unit seeks to ensure that policy prepared for consideration by the Prime Minister and Cabinet has clear goals, a robust assessment of costs and benefits, and clarity about how it will be implemented. The unit helps departments and agencies to prepare their implementation plans and to identify, assess and manage implementation risks. The unit also monitors the progress of the implementation of key government decisions and reports to the Prime Minister and Cabinet on the status of these decisions.

In 2009, the Prime Minister of **Malaysia** established the Performance Management and Delivery Unit in the Prime Minister's Department, which draws on both public and private sector officials to oversee both the government and economic transformation processes: "The Performance Management and Delivery Unit (PEMANDU) was formally established in 2009 and is a unit under the Prime Minister's Department. PEMANDU's main role and objective is to oversee the implementation, assess the progress, facilitate as well as support the delivery and drive

Box 2.6. **Implementation units in Australia, the United Kingdom and Malaysia** *(cont.)*

the progress of the Government Transformation Programme (GTP) and the Economic Transformation Programme (ETP). While the responsibility for end-to-end delivery of national key results areas and ministerial key results areas outcomes ultimately rests with the respective ministries, and the success of the national key economic areas rests with the private sector, PEMANDU has been mandated to catalyse bold changes in public and private sector delivery, support the ministries in the delivery planning process and provide an independent view of performance and progress to the Prime Minister and ministers" (PEMANDU, n.d.). Through PEMANDU, the government ensures effective implementation of its transformation initiatives against key performance indicators, while also drawing on private sector expertise to assist with the process of government and economic transformation.

*Source:* OECD (2012), *Slovenia: Towards a Strategic and Efficient State*, OECD Public Governance Reviews, OECD Publishing, Paris, http://dx.doi.org/10.1787/9789264173262-en.

Box 2.7. **Centre of government's role in preparing high-level government meetings**

One key management role of the CoG with respect to high-level government meetings is to ensure that harmonised consultation processes have been followed and that appropriate analytical tools have been used. The overall objective is to ensure that the usefulness and cost benefit of a particular action can be judged easily by the head of government and senior members of the government, whether they are knowledgeable in the field or not. Information should be presented in a way that allows political leaders to understand the need for – and consequences of – proposed policy interventions, to evaluate costs and benefits, to weigh evidence on their likely impact and to anticipate risks and resistance to policy.

Table 2.1 **Centre of government's role in reviewing items submitted to the Council of Ministers**

| | CoG reviews | CoG has authority to return items to ministry for additional work if criterion is not satisfied | This is reviewed by another body |
|---|---|---|---|
| That procedures for preparation and presentation are respected | 65% | 74% | 10% |
| That the item is in line with the government programme | 59% | 59% | 21% |
| That relevant ministries and other stakeholders have been consulted as required | 53% | 63% | 20% |
| Quality of legal drafting and legal conformity | 45% | 55% | 59% |
| That a regulation meets regulatory quality standards (public/economic benefits, that benefits outweigh costs, that an impact analysis has been carried out, etc.) | 43% | 64% | 43% |
| That adequate costing has been carried out | 41% | 48% | 62% |

*Source:* OECD (2014b), "Centre stage: Driving better policies from the centre of government", GOV/PGC/MPM(2014)3/FINAL, OECD, Paris, www.oecd.org/gov/Centre-Stage-Report.pdf.

## Recommendations

Beyond the administrative support for the Council of Ministers, the Ministry of the Presidency could play a more strategic role in supporting the quality of the decision-making process of the Council of Ministers, by reviewing agenda proposals on different dimensions. Such a review could cover a procedural check, a coherence check with the government's programme, a consultation check of relevant stakeholders, a legal conformity check, a regulatory standards check and a costing check. The balance between administrative and strategic support assured by the Ministry of the Presidency could subsequently also be reflected in its organisational chart, which would preferably remain stable across different government periods, in order to build and preserve capacity.

Explicit, and structural, investment in CoG capacity building should be considered, given the substantial turnover within CoG institutions (reflecting turnover in the Costa Rican public sector in general in line with the political cycle) on the one hand, and substantial challenges for successful CoG co-ordination, on the other hand. Primary beneficiaries for such training would be the Ministry of the Presidency and MIDEPLAN and could cover technical training, as well as soft skills like negotiation and communication skills. As an example, in Queensland, Australia, the government – via the Public Service Commission – has partnered with a university to run an Emerging Leaders Programme. Shared training for CoG actors could also foster a shared identity and culture across the public sector.

Costa Rica is by no means an exception in its struggle to deal efficiently and effectively with the institutionally decentralised sector. One way to move forward in this area would be to foster the CoG's strategic thinking about the institutionally decentralised sector. Across most OECD Members, governing public agencies is a challenge and is subject to numerous analytical and strategic reflections. Both cross-country analyses of agency governance tendencies and country-specific initiatives in this area could inspire Costa Rica and provide ideas for future action. At the level of cross-country analysis, it is worth mentioning "Governing public agencies in the 21st century" (Verhoest et al., 2011), which provides a solid inventory of international lessons and policy recommendations. Based on empirical research covering 30 countries, the report synthesises lessons learnt regarding the creation of agencies, their autonomy, the steering and control of agencies, agency management, and rationalisation and co-ordination. Some relevant elements for Costa Rica include reflections on the use of performance targets (to be used as opportunities to improve communication, exchange, negotiation and mutual learning) and the definition of agency performance (i.e. going beyond quantitative indicators, but also addressing quality, effectiveness, equal access and responsiveness). At the level of individual country experiences, Costa Rica could benefit from other countries' experiences in detailing a framework of how to deal with agencies. Interesting examples include the United Kingdom's "It takes two: How to create effective relationships between government and arm's-length bodies" (Rutter et al., 2012) or New Zealand's "Statutory Crown Entities – It Takes Three: Operating Expectations Framework" (Ministry for Culture and Heritage of New Zealand, 2014).

The government has made substantial efforts to strengthen the participatory dimension of the development of the NDP and is reflecting upon ways to make use of the NDP as a strategic policy document throughout the government's term. Next to strengthening the sector co-ordination though MIDEPLAN as one of the government's initiatives to achieve this goal, Costa Rica could also explore how to strengthen the ownership of the NDP and its 2030 strategy throughout its implementation. An interesting example in this respect is the case of Lithuania and its State Progress Council, which consists of 28 members, including government representatives, representatives of the parliament, the directors of 4 leading universities, business associations, the Head of the National Museum, non-governmental organisations (NGOs), academics, youth organisations, businesspeople and members of the business media. Each year, the State Progress Council assesses the relevance of the strategy initiatives, monitors the results and reports to the government. The monitoring occurs across three lines. First, a set of ten annual progress actions has been defined, the so-called "quick wins". Second, the consistent implementation of the strategy is ensured by means of strategic and planning documents, such as the National Progress Programme, which brings together national and EU funds. Furthermore, the "Progress report Lithuania" is part of the annual government report, and includes an assessment of the implementation of the annual progress actions, the 31 progress indicators and the results of progress forums. The direct involvement of communities and NGOs is the third line. The "Open Progress Forum" is a tool for thematically focused dialogue with society.

On the dialogue with citizens, and to make sure that citizen participation goes beyond the initial development of the NDP, Costa Rica could consider the development of consultation principles to be shared throughout the public sector. The United Kingdom's consultation principles[3] provide an interesting example in this respect. A guidance note sets out the principles that government departments and other public bodies should adopt for engaging stakeholders when developing policy and legislation. It is not a "how to" guide but aims to help policy makers make the right judgments about when, with whom and how to consult.

## Notes

1. Multi-level governance co-ordination is addressed in Chapter 7.
2. For the Budget of the Republic Act see: www.gaceta.go.cr/pub/2014/12/15/ALCA80A_15_12_2014.pdf.
3. The consultation principles are available at: www.gov.uk/government/uploads/system/uploads/attachment_data/file/255180/Consultation-Principles-Oct-2013.pdf.

## *References*

Alessandro, M., M. Lafuente and C. Santiso (2013). "The role of the center of government: A literature review", Institutions for Development, Technical Note, IDB-TN-581, Inter-American Development Bank, Washington, DC, http://publications.iadb.org/bitstream/handle/11319/5988/ICS%20TN%20The%20Role%20of%20the%20Center%20of%20Government.pdf?sequence=1.

Australian Government (2012), "Cabinet Implementation Unit", www.dpmc.gov.au/implementation/index.cfm.

Government of Costa Rica (2014), "Background report", unpublished working paper.

Ministry for Culture and Heritage of New Zealand (2014), "Statutory Crown Entities – It Takes Three: Operating Expectations Framework", Crown Copyright, www.ssc.govt.nz/sites/all/files/it-takes-three-operating-expectations-framework.pdf.

OECD (2014a), "Vision, leadership, innovation: Driving public policy performance", 33rd Meeting of Senior Officials from Centres of Government, OECD, Paris, www.oecd.org/gov/summary.pdf.

OECD (2014b), "Centre stage: Driving better policies from the centre of government", GOV/PGC/MPM(2014)3/FINAL, OECD, Paris, www.oecd.org/gov/Centre-Stage-Report.pdf.

OECD (2014c), *Kazakhstan: Review of the Central Administration*, OECD Public Governance Reviews, OECD Publishing, Paris, http://dx.doi.org/10.1787/9789264224605-en.

OECD (2013a), "Session notes", 32nd meeting of the Network of Senior Officials from Centres of Government, OECD, Paris, www.oecd.org/gov/COG-2013-Session-Notes-ENG.pdf.

OECD (2013b), *Colombia: Implementing Good Governance*, OECD Public Governance Reviews, OECD Publishing, Paris, http://dx.doi.org/10.1787/9789264202177-en.

OECD (2012), *Slovenia: Towards a Strategic and Efficient State*, OECD Public Governance Reviews, OECD Publishing, Paris, http://dx.doi.org/10.1787/9789264173262-en.

PEMANDU (n.d.), "About PEMANDU", http://www.pemandu.gov.my/about.aspx.

Rutter, J. et al. (2012), "It takes two: How to create effective relationships between government and arm's-length bodies", Institute for Government, London, www.instituteforgovernment.org.uk/sites/default/files/publications/it_takes_two_final_0.pdf.

UK Cabinet Office (2006), "Prime Minister's Delivery Unit", http://webarchive.nationalarchives.gov.uk/20060715142152/cabinetoffice.gov.uk/pmdu.

Verhoest, K. et al. (2011), "Governing public agencies in the 21st century: International lessons and policy recommendations", COST Office, KU Leuven, Public Management Institute, Leuven, Belgium, http://soc.kuleuven.be/io/cost/act/pdf/20110527_Brussels/COST_policy_brochure_for%20conference.pdf.

## *Further reading*

Ministry of National Planning and Economic Policy (2013), "Organigrama del Sector Público Costarricense", Ministry of National Planning and Economic Policy, San José, http://documentos.mideplan.go.cr/alfresco/d/d/workspace/SpacesStore/57787594-4413-4f0c-9ccd-b6a4e2f6d091/Organigrama%20del%20sector%20p%C3%BAblico%20costarricense%202013.pdf.

Republic of Costa Rica (1949), *Constitución Política de la Républica de Costa Rica*, www.constitution.org/cons/costaric.htm.

# Chapter 3.

# Monitoring and evaluation as a tool to become result-oriented in Costa Rica

*This chapter focuses on Costa Rica's national monitoring and evaluation system. Whereas a clear institutional set-up with a definition of roles and responsibilities for different actors has been developed, the country faces important challenges. These include the need to shift towards a result-oriented monitoring and evaluation culture, a lack of using performance information strategically, a weak alignment of the budget and policy cycle, and certain capacity constraints across the public sector. Recommendations are formulated to address these issues, including the promotion of a balanced set of result criteria, a balanced approach between accountability and learning objectives, further capacity strengthening, and promoting a gradual development of the monitoring and evaluation system.*

## The challenge of being result-oriented

Sound monitoring and evaluating of the performance and progress of public interventions implies the capacity to detect policy challenges, define adjustments to facilitate decision-making processes, feed strategic information into the decision-making process, and communicate in a timely manner to decision makers in order to achieve the expected goals of public interventions. In addition, strong monitoring and evaluation can foster transparency and accountability, and provide stakeholders with information regarding progress in the accomplishment of the government's goals and commitments.

However, modern policies are complex (both in design and impact) and strongly interdependent. Evidence, for instance under the format of indicators, is important to examine policy effects, learn from past experiences and inform decision making, though there is always a lurking risk of over-simplifying reality. In addition, the machinery of collecting and analysing evidence through a monitoring and evaluation system is not an end in itself and should not divert one from a strategic focus on the achievement of actual policy results.

As illustrated in Box 3.1, evidence-based decision making – for instance on the basis of monitoring and evaluation information – requires different elements to make sure that the "right evidence" is obtained, and used appropriately. Disposing of a good system of performance information does not yet imply thorough performance management. Performance management requires technical and political leadership, the capacity to feed performance information in the policy cycle and the versatility to adapt policies where needed.

## Legal framework

The National Planning Law No. 5525 of 1974 incorporates the reference to the mandate to evaluate systematically and permanently the results of the execution of plans, policies and programmes, with a pivotal role for the Ministry of National Planning and Economic Policy (*Ministerio de Planificación Nacional y Política Económica*, MIDEPLAN).

Executive Decree No. 23323 of 1994, amended by Executive Decree No. 33206 of 2006, confirms the main role of MIDEPLAN in evaluation, through the area of evaluation and monitoring. MIDEPLAN is responsible for accompanying sectors with the execution of the National Development Programme (NDP) and the fulfilment of the goal and priority actions through the provision of technical support and by strengthening co-ordination and communication among the institutions that are part of a sector, and for proposing evaluation processes and institutional reforms towards increased public efficiency.

Executive Decree No. 23720 of 1994 sets up the National Evaluation System (*Sistema Nacional de Evaluación*, SINE), co-ordinated by MIDEPLAN, as a planning tool to strengthen the managerial capacity of the civil service.

The constitutional reform of 2000 approved in Article 11 that: "The public administration, in the broad sense, shall be subject to a process of evaluation of results and accountability, with the consequent personal liability for officers in the performance of their duties. The law shall specify the means for this control of results and accountability to operate as a system covering all public institutions." Since 2000, the follow-up of this constitutional reform (i.e. the regulation of SINE by law) has not been addressed.

### Box 3.1. OECD experience regarding evidence-based decision making

Evidence-based policy analysis allows for decisions aimed at implementing and steering strategy to be taken in the country's medium- and long-term interests, based on evidence derived from strategic foresight and environmental scanning that correctly identifies domestic and international short- and long-term challenges and opportunities, on performance assessment that allows for judicious prioritisation of expenditures to achieve the best results with the least resources, and on individual issues being analysed within a broader strategic framework.

Throughout the OECD, good governance practice suggests that policy should be based on sound evidence derived from rigorous analysis of the available facts on the issue the policy is supposed to address. Governance practices determine how evidence contributes to identifying policy options and how rules are made. This evidence needs to be available at the right time and be seen by the right people. OECD practice suggests that the following major ingredients are needed to obtain and use the "right evidence":

- a sound methodology that allows for proper consideration of the immediate and long-term nature of the issue and of the rationale supporting different options for policy intervention (including doing nothing)
- good data for analysis
- public access to the data, assumptions and methodologies used to frame the issue and identify options to address it, so that scrutiny can be brought to bear and the analysis replicated independently
- time to carry out this analysis properly and to consult the general public on its results
- a capable and skilled public service including people skilled in quantitative methods
- a "receptive policy-making" environment – that is political leaders who are willing and able to decide on the basis of the evidence presented.

*Source:* Banks, G. (2010), "An economy-wide view: Speeches on structural reform", Australian Government Productivity Commission, Canberra, in: OECD (2013), *Public Governance Review of Poland: Implementing Strategic-State Capability*, OECD Publishing, Paris, http://dx.doi.org/10.1787/9789264201811-en.

The Financial Administration and Public Budgets Law No. 8131 of 2001 provides the basic framework regarding planning, financial administration and budgeting, defining relevant accountability and transparency mechanisms, as well as the notion of performance management. According to the law, public resource allocation and implementation shall respect three main principles: economy, efficiency and effectiveness, the three E's. Decision-making processes should be supported by timely and reliable information on the performance and situation of the public finances. The law also defines the NDP as the guiding framework for each institution's operational plans. Budgets shall be allocated based on the NDP, according to the financial situation of the government.

Executive Decree No. 32988 of 2006 regulates the monitoring and evaluation of the NDP in detail, specifying the need to define methodologies and instruments to be used in the process of evaluation. It also specifies the regular reporting on the NDP evaluation results, including addressees and timelines.

Executive Decree No. 35755 of 2010 establishes that MIDEPLAN is responsible for developing the NDP and for its systemic evaluation processes. In this regard, it shall:

- evaluate the progress of, and compliance with, the goals established in the NDP, in order to contribute to the decision-making processes
- perform special evaluations of strategic policies, plans, programmes and projects that are considered a priority
- guide the strategic evaluation through SINE, providing support and advice in the design of methodologies and guidelines
- strengthen the systematisation of information, with the objective of enhancing the credibility and reliability of public data
- disseminate the results of the evaluations in order to increase public transparency and accountability.

Executive Decree No. 37735 of 2013 regulates the planning system, establishing the co-ordination and management of the monitoring and evaluation of the results of the public policies as a function of the National Planning System (NPS). In addition, it creates the monitoring and evaluation sub-system and designates MIDEPLAN as the technical manager of the NPS, with the function of formulating the National Strategic Plan, the National Development Plan and the regional development plans, implementing mechanisms for their monitoring and evaluation. The decree also establishes technical and methodological guidelines aimed at improving the quality of the programming, execution, monitoring and compliance of the NDP's goals and of the national budget. Institutions should benefit from MIDEPLAN's technical and methodological assistance, which allows and promotes better programming, planning and budgeting. At the same time, the decree underlines that a strong link between institutional goals and the NDP strategic framework have to be kept. The decree also states that institutions receive feedback from the Comptroller General's reports on fiscal, financial and management practices that are submitted to the Legislative Assembly. Figure 3.1 synthesises the main legal framework for policy monitoring and evaluation in Costa Rica.

Figure 3.1. **Legal framework for policy monitoring and evaluation in Costa Rica**

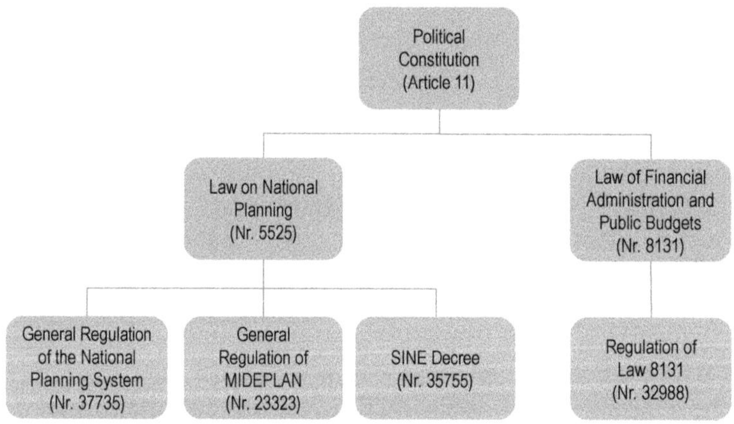


*Source:* Ministry of National Planning and Economic Policy (2013), "Lineamientos técnicos y metodológicos para la planeación y seguimiento a metas del Plan Nacional de Desarrollo; para la programación presupuestaria y para la evaluación estratégica en el sector público en Costa Rica" ("Technical and methodological guidelines for the planning and monitoring of goals of the National Development Plan; Guidelines for budget planning and strategic evaluation in the public sector in Costa Rica"), Ministry of National Planning and Economic Policy, San José, www.mag.go.cr/acerca_del_mag/circulares/planificacion-lineamientos-mideplan-.hacienda.pdf.

## Institutional framework

### *Key actors*

The National Evaluation System (SINE) is composed of the central government and includes the autonomous and semi-autonomous entities, the state-owned enterprises and the non-state public entities, insofar as they manage public funds. All these institutions, collect, organise and analyse information coming from the implementation of public programmes and projects in a co-ordinated way, to allow their monitoring and post-evaluation. Through the monitoring and evaluation of the NDP performed by MIDEPLAN and the other actors of SINE, progress or deviations from the plans are identified, creating the basis for the adoption of corrective actions when needed. Therefore, the regular, systematic and integral follow-up of the goals of the NDP seeks to provide relevant information for decision making to the authorities. Table 3.1 provides an overview of the main actors involved in the SINE framework.

Table 3.1. **Main actors in the SINE framework**

| Actor | Main functions in the SINE framework |
|---|---|
| President of the Republic | Political decision based on monitoring and evaluation reports on pre-established strategic priorities. |
| Ministry of National Planning and Economic Policy | SINE co-ordinator, responsible for issuing guidelines and leading the monitoring and evaluation processes. |
| Public institutions | Implementation, monitoring and evaluation of public policies, plans, programmes and projects, through its planning units. |
| Ministry of Finance | – Allocation of financial resources.<br>– Control over public expenditures (central government). |

*Source:* Ministry of National Planning and Economic Policy (2012a), "Manual gerencial para el diseño y ejecución de evaluaciones estratégicas de gobierno" ("Management manual for the design and execution of strategic evaluations"), Ministry of National Planning and Economic Policy, San José, http://documentos.mideplan.go.cr/alfresco/d/d/workspace/SpacesStore/9d96f810-3b89-4fd6-8701-d36327f02cc1/Manual_Gerencial_para_Dise%C3%B1o_Ejecucion_Evaluaciones_Estrategicas_Gobierno.pdf.

MIDEPLAN monitors the progress of, and compliance with, the goals established in the NDP in accordance with the National Planning Law, the Financial Administration and Public Budgets Law, and the Executive Decree setting up SINE. The ministry promotes continuous evaluation and modernisation of public services to address the needs of the citizens. In addition, it collaborates making proposals to fix national problems through the planning and performance evaluation in the public institutions. It submits two reports per year to the Comptroller General. The first describes the progress accomplished by each institution and sector until June. The second, "Annual NDP Goals Compliance Report", is presented by the end of the year.

### *National Evaluation System*

#### *Purpose and mandate*

As previously mentioned, SINE is defined as an instrument of the government to evaluate national development and the social welfare, by means of analysis, monitoring and evaluation of the results of the NDP and other planning instruments, promoting accountability and feedback.

The aim is to facilitate the definition of priorities, fund allocation and follow-up of the policy decisions taken, evaluating the result of strategic programmes and projects and the quality of the public delivery. In order to strengthen management, the executive annually selects a number of policies and plans with specific impact on the development of the country to be evaluated in detail. These evaluations are performed through SINE in addition to the evaluations of the NDP.

SINE is managed by MIDEPLAN, which co-ordinates the actions of the other ministries and institutions, as well as with sectors. MIDEPLAN elaborates and disseminates strategies, guidelines and methodologies for the monitoring and evaluation that are subsequently used by the various public entities involved (Box 3.2).

### Box 3.2. Examples of SINE guidelines and methodologies

**Management manual for the design and execution of strategic evaluations**

The handbook intends to be a management tool, allowing the institutions to identify the stages in the evaluation process, the approaches and methodological design that suit its implementation, the data analysis and the communication of results, *inter alia*. In addition, it incentivises the evaluation in the public sector, strengthens the technical capacities for strategic evaluation and therefore reinforces the democratic system, through increased transparency and accountability, as it provides timely and valid information.

The main goals of the manual are to:

- promote evaluation in the public entities
- increase the understanding of the evaluation process and the results
- define the conceptual and technical requirements for an evaluation that address the needs of the actors involved.

The manual underlines the importance of planning the evaluation process in an integrated way, involving five stages: programming, design, implementation, communication of the results and follow-up of the recommendations.

Additionally, the manual describes different methodological designs: quantitative approach, qualitative approach and mixed approach, which combines the two former. Finally, it describes the techniques for data collection, presentation of the results and follow-up processes.

**Guide for strategic evaluation of interventions in the public sector**

MIDEPLAN has taken its first steps in performing multi-disciplinary evaluations, in co-ordination with external evaluators. The guide was designed by MIDEPLAN for interested institutions to better structure their strategic evaluation proposals, to ease the prioritisation and selection process done by the monitoring and evaluation area. In addition, the manual intends to advise on strategic evaluation and to clarify to the institutions if its interventions might be subject to strategic evaluation, in relation with the information needs required. It also elaborates, *inter alia*, on the planning of the evaluation, the goals, the scope or the participants.

*Sources:* Ministry of National Planning and Economic Policy (2012a), "Manual gerencial para el diseño y ejecución de evaluaciones estratégicas de gobierno" ("Management manual for the design and execution of strategic evaluations"), Ministry of National Planning and Economic Policy, San José, http://documentos.mideplan.go.cr/alfresco/d/d/workspace/SpacesStore/9d96f810-3b89-4fd6-8701-d36327f02cc1/Manual_Gerencial_para_Dise%C3%B1o_Ejecucion_Evaluaciones_Estrategicas_Gobierno.pdf;
Ministry of National Planning and Economic Policy (2012b), "Guía para iniciativas de evaluación estratégica de intervenciones (políticas, planes, programas y proyectos) en el sector público" ("Guide for the strategic evaluation of interventions in the public sector (policies, plans, programmes and projects"), Ministry of National Planning and Economic Policy, San José, http://documentos.mideplan.go.cr:8080/ alfresco/d/d/workspace/SpacesStore/f6fef999-8dd1-411d-a348-4aefeacb98e2/Guia%20B3%20teoria%20intervencion.pdf.

SINE works through two transversal modules, which are interconnected and complementary:

- A self-evaluation module, aimed at developing a culture of evaluation at the institutional, sectorial and regional levels, including the follow-up of the priorities of the NDP and other relevant plans.
- A strategic evaluation module, aimed at evaluating policies, plans, programmes and projects of public interest determined in the NDP and other planning instruments, as a means to ensure the efficiency and transparency of public entities. MIDEPLAN advises on the strategies, guidelines and methodologies at its disposal. The public entities shall set up the monitoring and evaluation system according to the guidelines, to enrich strategic management.

So far the work has been focused on the second module, whereas the first one remains an issue to be addressed. In that sense, Costa Rica should continue working in building up a culture of self-evaluation, using the experiences of other countries.

*Structure*

A co-ordination unit within MIDEPLAN takes care of the following issues:

- provide feedback to line ministries and institutions on the results of the evaluations performed by MIDEPLAN
- provide training to improve the evaluation culture and its importance as a public management and accountability tool
- disseminate the main outcomes of the NDP evaluations
- elaborate methodologies
- disseminate and advise on the strategies, guidelines and methodologies issued by MIDEPLAN
- report on SINE in relation to the accountability of MIDEPLAN towards the executive and legislative branches
- evaluate policies or projects or particular interest for the government, when not included in the NDP.

Sectorial secretaries and institutional planning units act as liaison points within SINE, being partners of MIDEPLAN, under the supervision of the rector of a given sector. Their main activities are:

- put in place mechanisms to ensure the continuous monitoring and periodical assessment of the institutional plans in accordance with the NDP's priorities
- follow the guidelines and methodologies received from MIDEPLAN
- include in the monitoring and evaluation information regarding public investment projects linked to the NDP's goals and the National System of Public Investment (SNIP).

Finally, there are also co-ordination links with the Ministry of Finance, the Budgetary Authority and the Comptroller General.

### *Strategic objective*

SINE aims at ensuring the evaluation and accountability of the public sector towards citizens, in an objective, timely and transparent fashion, promoting:

- continuous improvement of public management, through the identification and programming of strategic actions, follow-up, assessment, feedback and benchmarking of good practices
- a culture of evaluation in the public sector, through the creation of internal evaluation systems within the institutions
- trustworthy and timely information to the authorities for the decision-making process
- the engagement of civil servants on transparency and accountability.

The system is meant to strengthen the managerial capacity in the public sector by the means of:

- measurement and promotion of timely and high-quality results of public actions, generation of quality data to increase the effectiveness and efficiency of public services, to ensure an economic, social and environmentally sustainable development
- information on monitoring and evaluation of the implementation of public policies and plans
- issuance of guidelines and methodologies of public evaluation, and advising.

### *Commitment to results*

SINE has put in place instruments to define the commitments of the institutions, such as the "commitment of results", which is an annual agreement for the institutional management, signed by the President of the Republic, the relevant authority and the Ministers of Planning and Finance, following a process of negotiation and ensuring a tight and permanent co-ordination between the various actors involved in the programming, management and resource allocation.

During the year, a follow-up of the "commitment of results" is carried out, as an important support for the institutions, facilitating the achievement of the goals at the end of the period. Specifically, every quarter institutions issue a follow-up report on the development of their actions, which contains data of the progress for each evaluation criteria, the difficulties encountered, the co-ordination or organisational problems, and other key elements. These reports are submitted to SINE, which elaborates an executive summary for the President and the concerned authorities, reflecting the situation and highlighting the actions that have been delayed, as well as those which have already been successfully achieved. Limitations and recommendations are also included. Each institution submits an annual evaluation report to SINE. SINE then elaborates a final report for the President and the authorities on the "commitments of results". This report includes a ranking of institutions, an analysis of the success factors and the difficulties of the process, as well as a detailed annex of achievements. Finally, the President publically recognises the institutional and sectorial performance, summarising the main results of the evaluation for the citizens.

## *FOCEVAL**

In 2009, the government of Costa Rica, in co-ordination with the academic sector, presented a proposal for international technical co-operation to improve evaluation capacities in the public sector, starting with MIDEPLAN. This initiative resulted in the programme FOCEVAL, in co-operation with the German government. FOCEVAL is a strategic partnership with a focus on raising awareness and promoting a culture of evaluation and transparency as a basis for public policy decision making. Promotion and training activities have been conducted at all levels as part of the programme, including for the central government, Congress, civil society representatives, programme and project directors, and public institutions that directly execute planning and monitoring and evaluation.

In the framework of FOCEVAL, pilot evaluations have been promoted. The entities proposed their own initiatives, thereby promoting a culture of learning and improvement. Four evaluations have been completed so far:

- evaluation of the methodological design of the NDP (MIDEPLAN)
- evaluation of the support to pedagogical management of schools with inclusive programmes (*Apoyo a la gestión pedagógica a centros educativos de calidad con orientación inclusiva*) (Ministry of Public Education)
- evaluation of the project Germinadora (Mixed Institute for Social Aid)
- evaluation of the Irrigation District Arenal-Tempisque.

## *Current monitoring and evaluation initiatives*

The government is currently reviewing its monitoring and evaluation activities, with the aim of strengthening the strategic added value of both activities.

### *Monitoring*

In order to foster strategic monitoring, a quarterly reporting mechanism is planned to be introduced for those NDP projects considered strategic in terms of their structural importance. A proposal has been formulated by MIDEPLAN, and presidential approval is pending. The reporting mechanism will focus on the accomplishments in relation to the annual target, the obstacles found and the risks foreseen to reach the proposed objective and how these are proposed to be managed, as well as the identification of specific support required from other sectors or institutions to accomplish the target. The report will have a qualitative approach and an emphasis on generating inputs for strategic decision making at the level of the Council of Ministers.

Semi-annual and annual monitoring will be oriented towards the accomplishments of quantitative targets and produced effects associated to planned results. The latter will be assessed according to qualitative criteria related to human development (gender gap reduction, transparency, poverty reduction, economic growth, labour market access and territorial gap decrease). As for the quarterly reporting, results should be presented to the President of the Republic in a Council of Ministers.

A workgroup has been formed including MIDEPLAN, the Minister of Finance and the Central Bank with the main objective to monitor 40 key projects that aim to improve competitiveness, close the infrastructure gap and boost the economy.

* See: www.foceval.org/.

The officials of the Sectorial Analysis Unit of the Development Planning Area of MIDEPLAN will give support to the meetings of the sectorial committees and shall promote an adequate articulation of the institutions forming the sector and the elaboration of the action plans. Furthermore, a programme is being created for strengthening the capacities of those officials in negotiation, political incidence, assertive communication and their respective areas of expertise. It is also intended to be a space to share good practices of the most successful sectors: environment and social development.

MIDEPLAN has drafted a decree, approved by the President, which prohibits the modification of goals in the NDP. In previous years, the goals were easily modified not only in the national targets but also in the specific programmes and projects. The decree states that only in cases of emergency or due to a direct impact from the global economy can the goals be modified. However, the decree also allows the institutions to justify non-compliance with the goals, giving the appropriate reasons.

#### *Evaluation*

The National Evaluation Agenda is formed by 13 projects, 7 of them corresponding to policies linked to poverty eradication and equity promotion. Evaluations of design, process, product and impact are planned. The evaluations on the Child Care Network (*Red de Cuido*), the National Directorate for Education and Nutrition Centres and Child Centres for Integrated Care (*Dirección Nacional de Centros de Educación y Nutrición y de Centros Infantiles de Atención Integral*, CENCINAI), the National Support Programme for Micro and Small Enterprises (*Programa Nacional de Apoyo a la Micro y Pequeña Empresa*, PRONAMYPE) and AVANCEMOS (Student Scholarships) have already started.

## Challenges for the monitoring and evaluation system

### *Addressing the missing links*

Whereas substantial efforts have been – and are being – made in strengthening the monitoring and evaluation system, it is essential to address some of the missing links in the system, in order to get the most out of the efforts made. These missing links start on the planning system side (e.g. about 60% of the ministries do not have a strategic plan according to information provided by MIDEPLAN, which weakens the adherence to strategic goal setting and adherence at the level of individual institutions) and culminate at the very end of the monitoring and evaluation cycle (e.g. lack of feedback mechanisms based on monitoring and evaluation information provided by public institutions).

### *Strategic use of performance information*

Although MIDEPLAN is entrusted with co-ordinating SINE and providing technical guidance on monitoring and evaluation procedures, past governments did not always rely on MIDEPLAN as a technical information repository; nor did they strengthen SINE as an institutional support network for research and strategic analysis. National monitoring and evaluation served basic accountability requirements, but were rarely used as input for the design and development of new policies. Whereas the current government displays an interest to do things differently, such an approach has not yet been rolled out, let alone institutionalised. Box 3.3 provides an example of a comprehensive approach to the strategic use of performance data for decision making from the United States and Box 3.4 focuses on communicating progress with an example from the Netherlands.

### Box 3.3. Performance dialogue in the US federal government

The Government Performance and Results Act (GPRA) was introduced in 1993 with the aim to foster the use of performance information among federal managers. However, its success remained limited. While it succeeded in introducing a stable performance planning and reporting framework, and putting performance centre stage, it did not succeed sufficiently enough in involving leadership and focusing on prioritisation or management. Consequently, the Bush administration introduced the Performance Assessment Rating Tool (PART; 2003-08), hoping to be able to overcome the shortcomings of the GPRA. Nevertheless, although PART focused more on programmes, and more data and information have been produced in the scope of these programmes, the use of the produced information remained limited.

The GPRA Modernisation Act was adopted in 2010 (enacted in 2011). It established performance improvement roles and responsibilities across all levels of government, a goal framework and performance reviews, and modernised performance reporting.

Regarding the performance responsibilities, a major innovation has been the establishment of a full-time Performance Improvement Council, which advances and expands the practice of performance management and improvement, by supporting the achievement of cross-agency and agency priority goals, as well as by creating opportunities for best practice exchange and capacity building.

The established goal framework consists of three groups of goals:

- The federal cross-agency priority goals (15 in total, at the time of writing), which are set by the President every 4 years, and reviewed quarterly by the Director of the Office of Management and Budget (OMB) and by the Performance Improvement Council. These goals are meant to increase the co-ordination on outcomes that cut across multiple agencies and focus on the impact through improved implementation.
- The agency priority goals (96 in total, at the time of writing), set by the agency heads every 2 years and reviewed quarterly by the respective agency's chief operating officer and the performance improvement officer, drive progress on near-term, implementation-focused priorities. They do not reflect every priority, but complement the broader set of goals included in the agency's strategic plan.
- The strategic goals and objectives (303 in total, at the time of writing), set every 4 years and reviewed strategically on an annual basis by agencies and the OMB, are supported by multiple strategies, programmes and performance indicators. The strategic objectives break down the broad strategic goals of an agency. There are about 10-30 strategic objectives for each major agency.

Performance assessment and reporting are essential for improving the usefulness of performance and programme information. The OMB states in its analytical perspectives for the fiscal year 2011: "The ultimate test of an effective performance management system is whether it is used, not the number of goals and measures produced" (OMB, 2010: 73) Thus, in the scope of the GPRA Modernisation Act, the performance information of agencies is put on a central website[1] with quarterly updates on priority goals, and annual updates on all goals. Furthermore, a government-wide list of programmes is set up, which is updated annually.

In addition, the review of the strategic goals and objectives synthesises available performance information and evidence to inform budget, legislative and management decisions. They are conducted by the agencies for each "strategic objective" in an agency's strategic plan. The reviews are designed to help meet the needs of leadership in identifying opportunities for reform proposals, executive actions, communication opportunities, etc. Furthermore, they synthesise a broad evidence and information base (indicators, evaluations, risk management, partner contributions, external factors, research, etc.) and prioritise findings for decision making. In addition, they make meaningful distinctions in performance, such as identifying areas of noteworthy progress and significant challenges. Finally, they incentivise organisations to develop a culture focused on learning and improving performance. Thus, they are both backward-looking, insofar as they evaluate, measure and report, which allows for learning and innovation, and forward-looking, insofar as they address improvement areas, risks and opportunities. Detailed agency guidance on the process is made available through www.whitehouse.gov/omb/circulars_all_current_year_all_toc (Part 6).

### Box 3.3. Performance dialogue in the US federal government (*cont.*)

These systematic and strategic goal-setting, reviewing and reporting mechanisms thus allow for better informed decision making and learning, which ultimately will improve outcomes and productivity. In more practical terms, some general lessons agencies have already learnt from this approach are:

- Breaking down silos: many agencies reported that the strategic review was the first time certain programmes met to discuss cross-cutting, strategic issues.
- Identifying evidence gaps: agencies were able to identify strategic objectives with relatively weak evidence and thus identify areas for improving metrics.
- Aligning activities to the strategic plan: agencies were able to begin aligning activities directly with strategic goals and objectives.
- Engagement: most agencies' performance staff were interested and engaged in finding value from strategic reviews. For instance, over 100 agency staff attended a strategic planning summit in March 2013, over 100 agency staff attended strategic review summits in both February and July 2014, and one performance improvement officer stated "it was the first time in 20 years that their programme staff had asked to participate in a performance management effort at the agency".

*Note:* 1. www.performance.gov.

*Sources:* Moynihan, D.P. and S. Lavertu (2012), "Does involvement in performance reforms encourage performance information use? Evaluating GPRA and PART", *Public Administration Review*, Vol. 72, No. 4, pp. 592-602; Mirza, A. (2014), "Improving government performance in the US", presentation made at Portugal-OECD seminar on "Strengthening ESIF Policy Indicators", Lisbon, 27-28 October.

### Box 3.4. Monitoring and communicating progress: "The Progress Overview" in the Netherlands

In order to show end-users how far measurable and tangible progress has been achieved, the Netherlands has developed a visible, at-a-glance overview of progress towards achieving 14 key quantitative and qualitative indicators linked to quantitative targets to reduce regulatory burdens on businesses. It uses the idea of dashboard dials to clearly present the targets and to what extent they have been achieved. Progress is measured against the three core aims of "less", "simpler" and "tangible":

- "less" includes targets about administrative burdens, substantive compliance costs, inspection burdens and subsidies
- "simpler" measures more reliable, transparent and faster results
- "tangible" tracks perceptions around the issues that business views as key irritants, linked to quantitative targets as well.

Additional information can be obtained in the Netherlands' progress report on regulatory burdens at: www.mg.gov.pl/NR/rdonlyres/D17C9179-B4B9-4DFE-B197-DCCBEFEE50D1/56432/Progress_Report_RB09.pdf.

*Source:* Ministry for Economic and Business Affairs (Denmark), Regulatory Reform Group (the Netherlands) and Department for Business, Innovation and Skills (United Kingdom) (2010), *Smart Regulation: A Cleaner, Fairer and More Competitive EU*, Copenhagen, The Hague and London.

### *Fine-tuning budget and policy monitoring*

There remain challenges in the field of the co-ordination of oversight bodies, stemming from the search for compatibility between the SINE methodologies and the more traditional budget monitoring. These include:

- time gap between the budget formulation process and the definition of strategic actions to be evaluated by SINE at the beginning of the year, once the budget has already been approved
- the variety of evaluation and control tools used by the oversight bodies
- the different reporting timing of the oversight bodies
- the limited feedback among the involved bodies
- the variety of methodological guidelines designed by different monitoring institutions, making it necessary to harmonise them, including agreements regarding project design, programming and performance evaluation.

There have been efforts to improve the situation, for instance, by creating the Technical Inter-institutional Commission of Planning, Programming and Evaluation of the Executive Branch (Ministry of Finance and MIDEPLAN) that in May 2014 issued "Technical guidelines for planning and monitoring" to orient the institutions on the different evaluation mechanisms. However, the two ministries collect information separately and for different purposes, which creates additional transaction costs, both between MIDEPLAN and the Ministry of Finance, and for the interaction between these two institutions and the sector institutions.

### *Capacity development*

Historically, MIDEPLAN has had an agenda for training and skills development. The ministry is currently undertaking a series of initiatives to strengthen this component of the evaluation and monitoring system, which needs further reinforcement across government.

Recently, and in order to consolidate the process of strategic evaluation, some short courses have been imparted to the personnel from the Evaluation and Monitoring Area of MIDEPLAN. Also, staff has worked closely with external evaluators performing particular evaluations and learning-by-doing. The ministry is defining occupational profiles that correspond to its activities and duties; additionally, it is identifying training needs and designing a training programme for MIDEPLAN's staff, as well as other institutions of SINE. These institutions have received training in the use of the "Management manual for the design and execution of strategic evaluations", as well as on information systems used to monitor the progress of the NDP goals.

Finally, the Ministry of Finance has imparted courses to the institutions under its influence in areas such as results/performance-based budgeting, programmatic structures and indicators, among others. However, and in line with MIDEPLAN's experience, there is a need for permanent training and skills development and for embedding the acquired skills in daily management practices.

## Recommendations

Costa Rica could further strengthen its efforts to shift from a process-oriented towards a result-oriented monitoring and evaluation culture. Such a shift implies a focus on results rather than on (reporting) compliance. It is important to underline that a "performance" orientation of an evaluation culture should not only focus on quantitative targets to achieve and performance criteria like economy or efficiency, but also incorporate criteria like quality, effectiveness, equal access (*cf.* for instance regional disparities) and responsiveness.

A shift towards a result-oriented monitoring and evaluation culture requires particular attention for the development of a balanced approach between "accountability" and "learning" objectives. A bigger emphasis on, and higher visibility of, result achievements can provoke counterproductive incentives to overrate performance/or and to focus on targets which are easy to achieve (i.e. lack of ambitious goal setting). Moreover, it risks suppressing the opportunity to learn from occasional weak performance and policy failures, if no room is left to make mistakes and learn from them. The monitoring and evaluation system should strike a balance between a focus on goal achievement on the one hand, and on understanding the "why" of good or bad performance on the other.

While expanding the monitoring and evaluation system, it is essential to keep a focus on strengthening capacity of all actors who are part of the monitoring and evaluation chain. This implies, amongst others, a strategic approach (across government) to capacity development for data collection, data analysis, reporting and communication, and use of data. It is important to acknowledge, for instance, that the supply of performance data does not imply that people know how to analyse and interpret the data and, subsequently, how to use the data. In addition, clear roles and responsibilities have to be assigned to different actors (i.e. suppliers and users of performance information). In order to ensure strategic resource allocation, it is important to develop a clear view of the hierarchy of goals, and appropriate timing and frequency for data collection and analysis.

Given the substantial investment of both financial and human resources in the process of strengthening the country's monitoring and evaluation system, it is important to provide incentives to all actors involved to use the data generated through the monitoring and evaluation system, i.e. empowerment to act on performance information. Such empowerment could be linked to the ability to revise (update) policy priorities and performance goals, identify corrective actions to address observed problems (including budgetary reallocation where needed), reward goal achievement, etc. Whereas roping in the institutionally decentralised sector is important to ensure achievement of strategic goals across government, it probably requires a different – and complementary – strategy to empower both the central government and institutionally decentralised actors.

Taking into account the country's ambitious goals to strengthen its monitoring and evaluation framework, it is important to allow for a gradual development of the system. Getting the system "up and running" (i.e. design the process, define the goals, identify the available monitoring and evaluation tools, detect capacity development needs, etc.) is a first step. Subsequently, it is possible to explore different "systemic goals" of the monitoring and evaluation system, which could gradually become more ambitious, e.g. measure performance, identify corrective measures, inform the budgetary process, incorporate risk assessments, etc. Each of these goals requires substantial resources and time to achieve. A particular point of attention is the development of a strategy on how to address cross-institutional goals. Such cross-institutional policy objectives tend to be numerous, whereas strengthening monitoring and evaluation objectives for individual institutions risks reinforcing a silo-based approach to policy making (i.e. focus on policy goals which can be achieved by an individual institution).

Citizen and stakeholder participation in the evaluation process could be promoted, through polls or focus groups carried out periodically, to explore the public's perception of the government's achievements.

## *References*


Banks, G. (2010), "An economy-wide view: Speeches on structural reform", Australian Government Productivity Commission, Canberra, in: OECD (2013), *Public Governance Review of Poland: Implementing Strategic-State Capability*, OECD Publishing, Paris, http://dx.doi.org/10.1787/9789264201811-en.

Ministry for Economic and Business Affairs (Denmark), Regulatory Reform Group (the Netherlands) and Department for Business, Innovation and Skills (United Kingdom) (2010), *Smart Regulation: A Cleaner, Fairer and More Competitive EU*, Copenhagen, The Hague and London.

Ministry of National Planning and Economic Policy (2013), "Lineamientos técnicos y metodológicos para la planeación y seguimiento a metas del Plan Nacional de Desarrollo; para la programación presupuestaria y para la evaluación estratégica en el sector público en Costa Rica" ("Technical and methodological guidelines for the planning and monitoring of goals of the National Development Plan; Guidelines for budget planning and strategic evaluation in the public sector in Costa Rica"), Ministry of National Planning and Economic Policy, San José, www.mag.go.cr/acerca_del_mag/circulares/planificacion-lineamientos-mideplan-.hacienda.pdf.

Ministry of National Planning and Economic Policy (2012a), "Manual gerencial para el diseño y ejecución de evaluaciones estratégicas de gobierno" ("Management manual for the design and execution of strategic evaluations"), Ministry of National Planning and Economic Policy, San José, http://documentos.mideplan.go.cr/alfresco/d/d/workspace/SpacesStore/9d96f810-3b89-4fd6-8701-d36327f02cc1/Manual_Gerencial_para_Dise%C3%B1o_Ejecucion_Evaluaciones_Estrategicas_Gobierno.pdf.

Ministry of National Planning and Economic Policy (2012b), "Guía para iniciativas de evaluación estratégica de intervenciones (políticas, planes, programas y proyectos) en el sector público" ("Guide for the strategic evaluation of interventions in the public sector (policies, plans, programmes and projects"), Ministry of National Planning and Economic Policy, San José, http://documentos.mideplan.go.cr:8080/alfresco/d/d/workspace/SpacesStore/f6fef999-8dd1-411d-a348-4aefeacb98e2/Guia%20B3%20teoria%20intervencion.pdf.

Mirza, A. (2014), "Improving government performance in the US", presentation made at Portugal-OECD seminar on "Strengthening ESIF Policy Indicators", Lisbon, 27-28 October.

Moynihan, D.P. and S. Lavertu (2012), "Does involvement in performance reforms encourage performance information use? Evaluating GPRA and PART", *Public Administration Review*, Vol. 72, No. 4, pp. 592-602.

OECD (2013), *Public Governance Review of Poland: Implementing Strategic-State Capability*, OECD Publishing, Paris, http://dx.doi.org/10.1787/9789264201811-en.

OMB (2010), "Analytical Perspectives", Budget of the U.S. Government, Fiscal Year 2011, Office of Management and Budget, Washington, DC, www.gpo.gov/fdsys/pkg/BUDGET-2011-PER/pdf/BUDGET-2011-PER.pdf.

## *Further reading*

Deutsche Gesellschaft für Internationale Zusammenarbeit (2013), "Programa FOCEVAL – Fomento de Capacidades en Evaluación en países seleccionados de Latinoamérica (FOCEVAL)" ("FOCEVAL Programme – Building of Evaluation Capacity in selected Latin American countries"), www.giz.de/en/downloads/giz2013-sp-evaluacion-foceval-latinoamerica.pdf.

# *Chapter 4.*

# Strengthening the budget framework for strategic planning in Costa Rica

*This chapter assesses Costa Rica's budgetary governance. Whereas the budget process is well institutionalised and regulated, a number of key challenges have been identified. Challenges include the fact that a large share of the budget falls outside the budgetary process headed by the Ministry of Finance, next to high budget rigidities, a lack of fiscal space and weak fiscal constraints. The chapter formulates recommendations in order to create and ensure fiscal space for government priority spending, align institutionally decentralised institutions with government priorities and ensure fiscal sustainability, allowing the country to finance and implement the priorities set out in the National Development Plan in a sustainable way.*

## From traditional to modern budgeting practices

Costa Rica has a distinctive political, legal and administrative governance framework born of a democratic tradition that values the social and economic rights of citizens that safeguard against excessive accumulation of power in the executive branch. In particular, Costa Rica was an early pioneer of comprehensive national planning, in keeping with the popular priority of identifying and advancing the social and economic interests of its citizens. However, Costa Rica finds it more and more challenging to finance and implement the priorities set out in the National Development Plan (NDP) with the available revenues. In addition, as the political system has matured with the passage of time, the framework has had the unintended effect of not just keeping the executive in check, but of constraining the system of government from effectively taking decisions.

Costa Rica made the most of traditional budget systems, and has reached the limits of what these traditional systems can achieve. It now needs to take a step forward and look at modern budgeting practices, for securing social and economic development. Costa Rica has taken its first steps towards programme budgeting and a medium-term expenditure framework (MTEF), but much work remains to be done. Today, the budget formulation process is very much driven by legal and constitutional requirements, in a traditional incremental process, which leaves little scope to include new programmes and government priorities in the budget.

The aim of this chapter is to suggest ways to allow the government to make sure that the priorities expressed in the NDP are actually financed and the corresponding programmes implemented, while ensuring long-term fiscal sustainability. The planning and budget processes will be analysed in the light of the Recommendation of the Council on Budgetary Governance, to identify areas of possible improvements and reforms (Box 4.1).

## Institutional setting

### *Actors involved in the national budget process*

The budget process in Costa Rica is well-institutionalised and regulated by the Constitution (Republic of Costa Rica, 1949) and Budget of the Republic Act. According to Article 176 of the Constitution, the national budget is issued for a one-year term from 1 January to 31 December. The budget process is supervised by the Ministry of Finance, and covers the executive branch (18 ministries), the Legislative Assembly, the Comptroller General, the Ombudsman Office, the judiciary and the Supreme Electoral Tribunal. The national budget does not cover the institutionally decentralised sector.

The annual budget is based on goals and priorities that must be linked to the NDP. It is prepared by the Ministry of Finance (National Budgetary Authority, *Dirección de Presupuesto Nacional*) and must comply with guidelines issued by the Budgetary Authority on budget policy, wage, employment, and investment and debt (Table 4.1).

The National Budgetary Authority is located in the Ministry of Finance. It is composed of four units of budget analysis; a unit of fiscal revenue and multi-annual programming; a monitoring unit of the budget execution; and a management unit. Each unit has between four and eight professionals and/or technicians.

### Box 4.1. Recommendation of the Council on Budgetary Governance

The OECD Principles of Budgetary Governance, which are embodied in the *Recommendation of the Council on Budgetary Governance*, draw together the lessons of a decade and more of work in the OECD Working Party of Senior Budget Officials (SBO) and its associated networks. The Recommendation provides a concise overview of good practices across the full spectrum of budget activity, taking account in particular of the lessons of the recent economic crisis, and aiming to give practical guidance for designing, implementing and improving budget systems to meet the challenges of the future. The overall intention is to provide a useful reference tool for policy makers and practitioners around the world, and help ensure that public resources are planned, managed and used effectively to make a positive impact on citizens' lives.

The Recommendation recognises that budgeting is not a standalone process, removed from the other channels of government action. Good budgeting is supported by, and in turn supports, the various pillars of modern public governance: integrity, openness, participation, accountability and a strategic approach to planning and achieving national objectives. Budgeting is thus a keystone in the architecture of trust between states and their citizens.

1. Manage budgets within clear, credible and predictable limits for fiscal policy.
2. Closely align budgets with the medium-term strategic priorities of government.
3. Design the capital budgeting framework in order to meet national development needs in a cost-effective and coherent manner.
4. Ensure that budget documents and data are open, transparent and accessible.
5. Provide for an inclusive, participative and realistic debate on budgetary choices.
6. Present a comprehensive, accurate and reliable account of the public finances.
7. Actively plan, manage and monitor budget execution.
8. Ensure that performance, evaluation and value for money are integral to the budget process.
9. Identify, assess and manage prudently longer term sustainability and other fiscal risks.
10. Promote the integrity and quality of budgetary forecasts, fiscal plans and budgetary implementation through rigorous quality assurance including independent audit.

*Source:* OECD (2015), *Recommendation of the Council on Budgetary Governance*, OECD, Paris, http://acts.oecd.org/Instruments/ShowInstrumentView.aspx?InstrumentID=319&InstrumentPID=347&Lang=en&Book=False.

### Table 4.1. Actors involved in the national budget process

| | |
|---|---|
| Ministry of National Planning and Economic Policy (Ministerio de Planificación Nacional y Política Económica, MIDEPLAN) | Prepares the National Development Plan which guides the budget |
| National Budgetary Authority, Dirección General de Presupuesto Nacional – Ministry of Finance | Prepares the annual budget and issues a medium-term fiscal framework (current year plus four years) for the central government |
| Budgetary Authority (Autoridad Presupuestaria) | Issues "guidelines" on budget policies, wage, employment, debt and investment matters |
| Technical Secretariat of the Budgetary Authority (Secretaría Técnica de la Autoridad Presupuestaria, STAP) – Ministry of Finance | Provides technical reports to support the discussions and decisions of the Budgetary Authority |
| Central Bank | Prepares macroeconomic assumptions |

The Budgetary Authority is a collegiate body, which is not common in OECD Members. It is comprised of the Minister of Finance (chair), the Minister of Planning and the Minister of the Presidency (or their vice-ministers which can replace them). The Budgetary Authority meets once a month and holds extraordinary sessions when required. It issues "guidelines" (*lineamientos*) on public wages (based on the negotiations with the unions), public employment, budget policies (decisions to increase expenditure ceilings), investment and debt (any public institution needs the approval of the Budgetary Authority to issue debt). These guidelines must be approved by the President of the Republic, and are used by the National Budgetary Authority when preparing the national budget.

The Budgetary Authority is served by the Technical Secretariat of the Budgetary Authority (*Secretaría Técnica de la Autoridad Presupuestaria*, STAP), located in the Ministry of Finance. The STAP prepares reports which are submitted to the Budgetary Authority. Based on these reports, the Budgetary Authority takes decisions, which are communicated to and applied by the relevant institutions.

### *The institutionally decentralised public sector*

Costa Rica is characterised by a high degree of institutional decentralisation. Institutional decentralisation is understood as the transfer of planning, managing, funding and resource allocation responsibilities from the central government to different types of autonomous institutions.

The institutionally decentralised public sector is supervised by the Comptroller General, who approves its budgets. According to Law 8131, the entities which are within the scope of the Budgetary Authority must submit a copy of their budgets to the STAP. There are approximately 100 institutions under the scope of the Budgetary Authority, which belong to different institutional classifications. For the institutions under its responsibility, the STAP verifies compliance with the budgetary guidelines and provides a copy of its report to the Comptroller General. The Comptroller General must consider the review of the STAP as part of its budgetary approval.

The Comptroller General does not check whether the goals, objectives and expected results of the institutionally decentralised sector are in line with the NDP. The Ministry of National Planning and Economic Policy (*Ministerio de Planificación Nacional y Política Económica*, MIDEPLAN) is in charge of verifying that the entities comply with the NDP's goals and objectives, but does not have instruments to enforce this. Other countries, however, have put in place mechanisms and instruments to ensure compliance. Box 4.2 describes cost control mechanisms of independent agencies in France and the United Kingdom.

## Main challenges for budgeting and planning in Costa Rica

### *High budget rigidities and lack of fiscal space*

One of the main challenges identified by the Costa Rican authorities for conducting public policy and aligning the budget with the NDP is that a large share of the budget (about 50% of total consolidated general government spending) falls outside the budget preparatory process headed by the Ministry of Finance. However, when comparing the share of public expenditure included in the national budget in Costa Rica with practices in OECD Members, it appears that Costa Rica is quite in line with OECD practices. The main challenges may therefore lie elsewhere, and this section aims to identify the major blockages in the Costa Rican budget process, in order to concentrate reform efforts on the most relevant factors.

## Box 4.2. Alternative approaches to cost control in independent agencies

### The French approach

In the context of the French spending review procedure, initiated under the Sarkozy presidency, France has put up a list of all central government institutions outside the state, called "*operateurs d'État*" (state operators). These institutions have legal personality and are thus public non-profit institutions. Their legal status can vary: they can have several forms of public legal personality ("*établissement public administratif*", "*établissement public industriel et commercial*", "*groupement d'interet public*") or of private legal personality (foundations, associations). In total, some 650 institutions were identified. They can be divided in groups of institutions of the same kind, such as universities and cultural institutions (museums, theatres, etc.) and unique institutions.

In a first stage, the French government has started to apply rules of operational management to all institutions on the list. Although the state operators have legal personality and thus own their own resources, they are dependent on public financing, so that rules of operational management can be imposed on them via conditionalities attached to the public grants. However, in France, there exist also a large number of agencies that have no legal personality and still enjoy a large degree of autonomy in virtue of their legal status as "*services à competences nationales*" (SCN, services with national competences) and "*autorités administratives indépendentes*" (AAI, independent administrative authorities). These agencies thus far escaped the rules imposed on state operators. For this reason the French government has now embarked on a broader approach that covers not only the state operators but also the SCNs and the AAIs. In the context of this broader approach, the French word "*agences*" is now used to denote the entire spectre of independent agencies and public non-profit institutions. The basic idea is that all these institutions will be subjected to the same rules of operational management, which will be stricter than the regime previously applied to the state operators. Moreover the new regime will require that core ministries develop a clear policy of operational management and financing ("*tutelle*") for the institutions under their umbrella and become accountable for the results of this policy. Recent policy documents recognise that thus far there are no clear policies or criteria in place that determine which legal form publicly financed institutions should take (SCN, AAI or a variety of forms under public and private law with legal personality). This is seen as problematic and efforts are underway to develop a more systematic approach in this respect.

### The United Kingdom approach

In the United Kingdom, the government started in the early 1990s with an operation to devolve many executed tasks to agencies at arm's-length distance from the government, the so-called "Next Steps agencies" named after the Next Steps policy document of the Thatcher Cabinet. This initiative provided inspiration to many governments of other OECD Members to start similar initiatives. The new agencies existed henceforth next to many other public bodies that already had a semi-autonomous status in virtue of legal and administrative provisions of earlier decades or even centuries.

As a consequence, the domain of public bodies grew substantially, and it was not always clear which criteria were used for the attribution of the various forms of legal and administrative status.

The British government continues to work to provide greater clarity in the way in which it classifies arm's-length and independent agencies. In 2011, the Cabinet Office published a guide for ministries on the categorisation of public bodies. This guide was revised in December 2012. Moreover, in 2010, the UK government undertook a review of public bodies, encompassing 900 public bodies across 17 ministries, which will lead to the abolition, merger or substantial reform of approximately 500 bodies. Currently, the government distinguishes a range of categories of public bodies. Among these three key models are: 1) non-ministerial departments; 2) executive agencies; and 3) non-departmental public bodies (NDPBs).

Box 4.2. **Alternative approaches to cost control in independent agencies** (*cont.*)

Non-ministerial departments are departments (ministries) not headed by a minister but usually headed by a statutory board. They are accountable to parliament through their sponsoring ministers, but have their own budget voted directly by parliament. Examples are the Food Standards Agency, HM Revenues and Customs, the Office for Standards in Education, Children's Services and Skills. They date from the time before the executive agencies. In view of their privileged position, it has become difficult to turn them into executive agencies.

Executive agencies are part of a government department (ministry). They originated from the Next Steps initiatve. They carry out a range of executive tasks, with policy (including executive policy) set out by ministers. They are part of a government ministry and have no separate legal personality. Examples include: HM Passport Office, Maritime and Coastguard Agency.

Non-departmental public bodies comprise four types: 1) executive; 2) advisory; 3) tribunal; and 4) independent monitory boards. Examples of executive non-departmental public bodies are the Arts Council England, the British Council, the Information Commissioner, the Parole Board. Executive non-departmental public bodies are often established as statutory bodies or as companies. Examples are the Advisory Committee on the Misuse of Drugs, the Boundary Commissions (advising on Constituency Boundaries). Examples of tribunal non-departmental public bodies are the Foreign Compensation Commission and the Traffic Commissioners. Examples of the independent monitoring boards are the Independent Monitoring Board of Prisons, the Independent Monitoring Board of Immigration Removal Centres and the Independent Monitoring Board of Immigration Holding Facilities.

Executive non-departmental public bodies are often established as statutory bodies or as companies (with legal personality), whereas the other types of non-departmental public bodies are not. Non-departmental public bodies are usually financed by their parent ministry. It is government policy to reduce the size of the non-departmental public body sector. All such bodies will be subjected to a review of control and governance arrangements every three years which will: 1) provide a robust challenge to the continuing need for individual non-departmental public bodies, both their function and form; 2) if it is decided that a body should be retained as a non-departmental public body, ensure that the body is complying with recognised principles of good corporate governance.

In making the case for a new non-departmental public body, departments must assess the function or activity against the following tests: 1) is this a technical function (which needs external expertise to deliver); 2) is this a function which needs to be, and be seen to be, delivered with absolute political impartiality (such as certain regulatory functions); 3) or is this a function which needs to be delivered independently of ministers to establish facts and/or figures with integrity and credibility.

It is characteristic for the UK approach: 1) that agencies that in virtue of legal provisions have a certain autonomy in their executive policy (non-departmental public bodies and non-ministerial departments, independent agencies) are fully accountable for their costs to ministers, regardless whether they have legal personality; 2) that strict criteria are used for the establishment of the various types of arm's-length and independent agencies and that efforts are made to change the administrative or legal status of existing bodies in line with these criteria.

*Source*: OECD (2014a), Building on Basics, Value for Money in Government, OECD Publishing, Paris. http://dx.doi.org/10.1787/9789264235052-en.

Using financial information consolidated by institutional classification for general government, central government (i.e. national budget) expenditure represents 50% of total general government expenditure in Costa Rica.[1] While this number may still not be perfectly comparable to OECD National Accounts information,[2] it can be noted that it is slightly over the OECD average, as in OECD Members central government represents on average 46.3% of general government expenditure.[3] The remainder represents expenditure by the sub-national governments (state and local) and by social security institutions. In very decentralised Members such as Belgium, Canada, Germany, Spain or Switzerland, the share of central government controlled expenditure is below 30% of general government expenditure (and as low as 15% in Switzerland). This, of course, requires strong governance instruments to co-ordinate government policies across levels of government and social security institutions, as well as monitoring and evaluation tools.

In Costa Rica, the room for manoeuvre of the budget is very limited. About 95% of central government expenditures are pre-assigned. Indeed, an important share of the budget consists of mandatory spending such as interest payments or wages, over which the government has little control in the short run. While this is also the case in most OECD Members, Costa Rica also has a high share of earmarked revenues and expenditure. Indeed, more than half of central government spending is constrained by constitutional and legal mandates (Table 4.2). For example, the Political Constitution of Costa Rica states that at least 6% of ordinary revenues (*ingresos ordinarios*) shall be allocated to the judiciary power, and 8% of GDP to education. Only Brazil faces such a high share of pre-assigned expenditure (OECD/IDB, 2014).

Table 4.2. **Earmarked funds and mandatory expenditure in the 2014 national budget**

| | Billions colones (CRC) | Share (%) | Share of GDP (%) |
|---|---|---|---|
| Total budgeted expenditure | 6 649 | 100.0 | 24.7 |
| By constitutional mandate | 2 290 | 34.4 | 8.5 |
| By legal mandate | 1 497 | 22.5 | 5.6 |
| Mandatory expenditure | 2 528 | 37.9 | 9.4 |
| Debt service | 1 933 | 29.1 | 7.2 |
| Interests | 774 | 11.6 | 2.9 |
| Amortization | 1 159 | 17.4 | 4.3 |
| Wages (excl. Min of Education and Judicial power) | 585 | 8.8 | 2.2 |
| Other expenditure[1] | 344 | 5.2 | 1.3 |

*Note:* 1. Includes expenditure on goods and services, capital expenditure, transfers to deconcentrated agencies and public enterprises.

*Source:* Ministry of Finance (2013), "Marco fiscal presupuestario de mediano plazo, 2013-2018" ("Medium-term fiscal framework, 2013-2018"), Dirección General de Presupuesto, San José, www.hacienda.go.cr/docs/52224ab8cd313_MARCO%20PRESUPUESTARIO%20MEDIANO%20PLAZO%202013_2018.pdf.

Special-purpose funds and earmarking of revenues for particular purposes should be kept to a minimum (*Recommendation of the Council on Budgetary Governance*, Principle 7), as this does not allow governments to reorient resources to the priority sectors, and reduces the role of the budget as an instrument to support government policy.

The impact of budget earmarks on policy making and fiscal outcomes depends on the aggregates they are based on. Earmarked revenues reduce the budget room for manoeuvre, but are less of a threat to fiscal sustainability. In contrast, budget floors based on gross domestic product (GDP) – with no relation to revenue collection – are more problematic from the fiscal sustainability point of view. In addition, as expenditures are indexed on different macroeconomic variables, which may not evolve in parallel (some are indexed on revenues and others on GDP, for example), this may lead to distortions in the relative allocation of funds. For example, if a tax reform increases the tax-to-GDP ratio, this would increase the budget allocation of expenditure areas indexed on revenues, relative to those indexed on GDP. As far as priorities are concerned, if the budget earmarks apply to broad aggregates (education, justice), and are in line with national priorities, there should still be room to select priorities within each of these sectors.

Given the important rigidities in the budget allocation (earmarked revenues, spending floors), it would be important to have some flexibility in the execution of the budget. However, ministries do not have much flexibility to reallocate spending across line items. Reallocation is made through executive decrees, and it can only be done within a same programme. Reallocations between programmes are not allowed, as in resources assigned for capital purposes; in these cases, approval from the Congress is necessary. Reallocations between ministries must also be approved by the Congress. The ability of line ministries to carry over unused funds is also limited in Costa Rica, both in comparison with Latin American and Caribbean (LAC) and OECD Members (OECD/IDB, 2014).

In addition, tax revenues to GDP are low in Costa Rica compared to OECD Members, but also relatively low compared to other LAC countries. According to OECD Revenue Statistics, tax revenues represent only 21% of GDP in Costa Rica, while the LAC average is 27.9% and the OECD average 41.9% (OECD, 2014b). However, given the high level of revenue earmarks, increasing tax pressure alone would not provide a proportional additional fiscal space for financing government priorities. If budget earmarks are not reformed, increasing tax revenues to GDP would automatically increase the budget allocations which are tied to these, in a way that may not reflect government priorities (unless these spending floors are not binding, with actual spending above the minimum required floor). For example, 6% of revenues must be allocated to the judiciary power. If the ratio of tax revenues to GDP increased, this would increase the share of spending in judiciary power to GDP. As other budget items such as education are earmarked to the GDP, with no relation to revenues, increasing tax pressure would increase the relative share of spending in the judiciary compared to education.

### *Weak fiscal constraint*

Principle 1 of the *Recommendation of the Council on Budgetary Governance* states that budgets should be managed with clear, credible and predictable limits for fiscal policy. At minimum, governments should have a stated commitment to pursue a sound and sustainable fiscal policy.

Articles 176 and 179 of the Political Constitution of Costa Rica state that public finances should be balanced and sustainable, and provide tools for this. The first article states that: "the ordinary budget of the republic includes all the estimated revenues and all the expenditure authorised by the public administration during the economic year. Under no circumstances could the value of budgeted expenditure exceed the value of the estimated revenues". Article 179 also states that: "the Congress cannot increase the amount of expenditure budgeted by the executive, unless it specifies the new revenues which shall finance these, and for which the Comptroller General will have issued a report on the fiscal effectiveness of these".

In practice though, these two articles are not applied, and Costa Rica has no effective fiscal constraint, nor any mechanism for facilitating and enforcing medium-term fiscal discipline in the central government budget. This results in systematic budget deficits. Costa Rica's budget deficit is amongst the largest in the LAC region, and it is one of the few countries where the deficit did not decrease between 2009 and 2011 (Figure 4.1). Only Jamaica and Barbados have larger budget deficits than Costa Rica.

Figure 4.1. **General government fiscal balance as a percentage of GDP in Latin American countries**

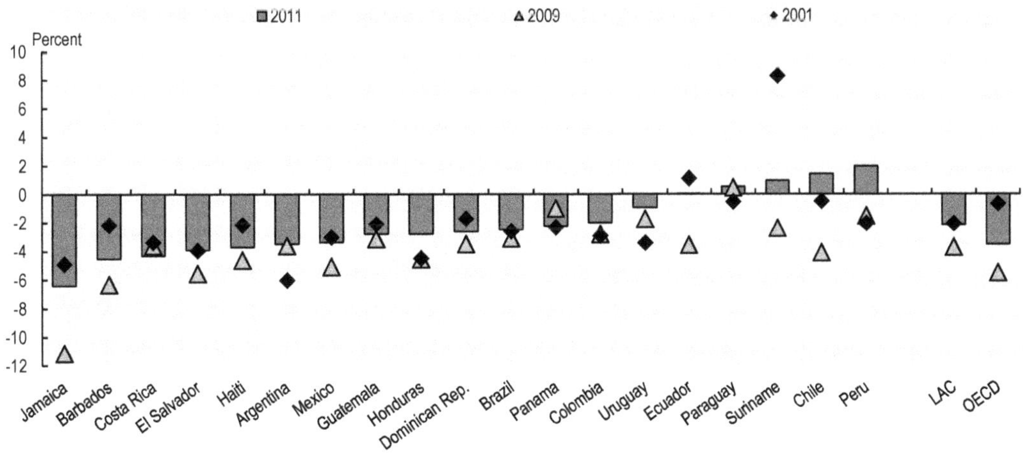


*Note:* LAC (Latin American and Caribbean).

*Source:* OECD/IDB (2014), *Government at a Glance: Latin America and the Caribbean 2014: Towards Innovative Public Financial Management*, OECD Publishing, Paris, http://dx.doi.org/10.1787/9789264209480-en. Data based on IMF, *World Economic Outlook Database* (October 2013). Data for OECD average: OECD National Accounts, "Valuation of public debt: Nominal value".

Costa Rica could recommit to fiscal discipline by reactivating the well-designed constitutional requirements that have no legal reality at present. This could take the form of a fiscal responsibility law, in the light of modern experience with fiscal rules. Fiscal rules typically cover revenue, expenditure, budget balance or debt (Box 4.3).

Box 4.3. **Fiscal rules in Latin American countries**

During the last decade, several Latin American and Caribbean (LAC) countries have implemented fiscal responsibility laws to improve the sustainability and transparency of fiscal policy, and to increase macroeconomic stability. As part of this, some countries have implemented fiscal rules that place long-term restrictions on fiscal policy through explicit numeric limits on fiscal aggregates.

The majority of LAC countries favour budget balance rules, which can be in terms of the overall balance, structural balance or cyclically adjusted balance. These rules mainly help to reduce budget discretion and ensure debt sustainability. LAC countries have also implemented expenditure rules, mainly to limit the size of government, and can be placed on total, primary or current expenditure. Debt rules are less prevalent, although they are very effective at limiting public indebtedness and ensuring the long-term sustainability of fiscal policy. The majority of these rules are founded on primary or secondary legislation. Revenue rules have not been implemented by any LAC country. Seven countries have not yet implemented any kind of fiscal rule. This is in stark contrast to the prevalence of fiscal rules among OECD member countries, particularly among European Union countries, which have committed to adopting debt and balance rules and to enshrining them in their laws or constitutions.

In order to guarantee compliance, many countries have enforcement mechanisms in place

Box 4.3. **Fiscal rules in Latin American countries** *(cont.)*

outlining the procedures in the event of a deviation from the rule. By following explicit and transparent guidelines, governments are also able to circumvent the rule in a temporary and responsible manner, so as to not erode the credibility of the tool and the sustainability of fiscal policy.

Many LAC countries have opted for mechanisms in which the entity responsible for the overrun must implement corrective measures, or submit a proposal to the legislature outlining future steps to correct deviations from the fiscal rule.

*Source*: OECD/IDB (2014), *Government at a Glance: Latin America and the Caribbean 2014: Towards Innovative Public Financial Management*, OECD Publishing, Paris, http://dx.doi.org/10.1787/9789264209480-en.

A medium-term expenditure framework (MTEF) is an important tool in setting a basis for the annual budget. To be effective, an MTEF should have the following characteristics (*Recommendation of the Council on Budgetary Governance*, Principle 2):

- it should have real force in setting boundaries for the main categories of expenditure, for each year of the medium-term horizon
- it should be fully aligned with the top-down budgetary constraints agreed by government
- it should be grounded upon realistic forecasts for baseline expenditure (i.e. using existing policies), including a clear outline of the key assumptions used
- it should show the correspondence with expenditure objectives and deliverables from national strategic plans
- it should include sufficient institutional incentives and flexibility to ensure that expenditure boundaries are respected.

An MTEF can be enshrined in law or be established in a policy or strategy decided by the government through other arrangements. Almost all OECD Members have established an MTEF. In most cases, it is approved in the Cabinet (52% countries) or in the legislature (34% countries; OECD, 2014b).

In Costa Rica, the Ministry of Finance publishes annually a document entitled "Medium-term fiscal and budgetary framework" (*Marco fiscal presupuestario de mediano plazo*). This is an important baseline exercise, which details the forecasts of baseline expenditure based on existing policies, and clearly states the assumptions used. However, it does not fulfil all the conditions to be an operative MTEF. Indeed, as the government has no clear fiscal target, this document does not set boundaries for the main categories of expenditures. While it is very useful to inform debate about the possible consequences of no policy change, it does not set goals or bind policy.

The OECD calculates a composite indicator of the use of a medium-term perspective in the budget process (OECD, 2014b). This indicator contains ten variables that cover information on the existence of a medium-term perspective in the budget process, the number of years the estimates cover, the types of expenditures included in the frameworks, the possibility of carrying over unused funds from one year to the next and how those funds are monitored. LAC countries tend to have a smaller value of this composite indicator than OECD Members. According to the OECD definition, Costa Rica does not have an MTEF, and so the value of the indicator is zero.

## *Budget transparency and accountability*

Budget documents and data should be open, transparent and accessible (*Recommendation of the Council on Budgetary Governance*, principle 4). Clear, factual budget reports should be available to inform the key stages of policy formulation, consideration and debate, as well as implementation and review. All budget reports should be published fully, promptly and routinely, and in a way that is accessible to citizens. Accessibility requires not only that budget documents be available on line, in open data formats (which is the case for Costa Rica), but also that detailed budget information can be understood by citizens. Today, due to inconsistencies in the institutional classifications used by the different ministries, and the important number of different datasets provided, it is difficult to create a link between objectives, goals, indicators and available resources.

### *Institutional classification*

The classification of the institutionally decentralised public sector used by MIDEPLAN is not consistent with the one used by the rest of the public sector. Improving the link between the plan, the budget and the results requires unifying these classifications.

MIDEPLAN classifies the institutionally decentralised public sector into:

- autonomous and semi-autonomous institutions
- state-owned public enterprises
- non-state-owned public enterprises
- non-state public entities.

However, according to the Financial Administration Act of the Republic and Public Budgets, which constitutes the legal framework for the definition and implementation of the institutional classifier of the public sector, the classification is composed of:

- decentralised non-business institutions
- decentralised bodies
- non-financial public corporations
- central government
- local governments
- financial public corporations.

Each of these institutional classifications contains one or more categories of the institutions mentioned above.

Budget documents and data are available on the Ministry of Finance's website. For the 2014 National Budget, the Ministry of Finance published the document "Citizens budget" to facilitate its understanding. However, financial information is provided under different consolidation methods: consolidated for the whole of public sector or only for general government, and within the consolidation for the whole of public sector, there are three different classifications: by function, by institution or by sector. Each of these data sets provides different values for important aggregates, such as central government expenditure or total public expenditure (and differences are sometimes very significant).

While these different methodologies can be explained and the differences between the values understood, it is difficult for the user to know what information is available, and which one to use. Providing a unique set of financial information – or at least putting one forward – would greatly improve transparency. To increase comparability with OECD data, information consolidated by general government should be privileged.

The Comptroller General produces several annual reports concerning the budgetary process that are available to the public. It has a System of Information and Plans and Budgets (*Sistema de Información de Planes y Presupuestos*) which is available on line. This system provides information on revenues, expenditures and results, year by year and institution by institution. It is not clearly stated in the system, but given its purpose, it seems that information is provided on a non-consolidated basis. Indeed, the aim of this system is to allow users to monitor the execution of budgeted funds, institution by institution, and year by year. It is not meant to build a series of revenues and expenditures over a few years for the different institutions composing the public sector.

A related issue concerns the limited flexibility that budgets have due to the weight of permanent legislation. There are a number of tools and procedural rules that can make the fiscal examination of permanent legislation more rigorous. Legislative proposals that have a fiscal impact tend to be formally approved or endorsed by the Ministry of Finance, and analysed separately by parliamentary finance committees; in some countries, members of parliament can only vote up or down but not comment on proposals from the executive that have a fiscal impact; independent fiscal institutions may be called upon to provide independent estimates of the fiscal implications of proposed legislation; implementation of legislation may be conditional on the availability of resources with the possibility of government postponing it if there is not appropriate funding, or legislation may include provisions to adjust to key parameters to ensure fiscal sustainability (Marcel, 2014). In Colombia, for example, the Superior Council on Fiscal Policy (*Consejo Superior de Política Fiscal*, CONFIS) plays an important role in evaluating legislation or projects which have financial impact on future budgets (Box 4.4).

### Box 4.4. The key role of the Superior Council on Fiscal Policy in Colombia

In Colombia, the Superior Council on Fiscal Policy (*Consejo Superior de Política Fiscal*, CONFIS) plays an important role in ensuring the fiscal sustainability of public finances.

CONFIS is a body related to the Ministry of Finance and Public Credit. It is responsible for managing the fiscal policy and co-ordinating the budget system of Colombia. CONFIS is composed of the Minister of Finance and Public Credit (who chairs it), the Director of the National Planning Department (DNP), the Economic Counsellor of the Presidency of the Republic, the Vice Ministers of Finance, the Director of the General Department of the National Treasury and Public Credit and of Taxes and Customs.

All legislation creating future expenditure obligations for the government must be summited to and approved by CONFIS. CONFIS evaluates, modifies and approves the Financial Plan of the Public Sector, analyses the financial implications of the Annual Operational Investment Plan, determines the fiscal targets, and approves and modifies, via resolutions, the budgets of industrial and commercial public enterprises and mixed economy enterprises.

*Source*: OECD (2013), *Colombia: Implementing Good Governance*, OECD Public Governance Reviews, OECD Publishing, Paris, http://dx.doi.org/10.1787/9789264202177-en.

### *Co-ordination with the institutionally decentralised sector*

As a contract of trust between citizens and the state, it is expected that the budget document should account comprehensively and correctly of all expenditures and revenues of the national government (*Recommendation of the Council on Budgetary Governance*, Principle 4). Principle 2 of the *Recommendation of the Council on Budgetary Governance* states that budgets should be closely aligned with the medium-term strategic priorities of government. To promote alignment with the multi-year planning, prioritisation and goal-setting functions of government, the budget process should organise and structure budget allocations in a way that corresponds readily with national objectives.

As the funding schemes of the institutionally decentralised sector are rigid, the government cannot reallocate funds from one spending area to another according to its priorities. In addition, the institutionally decentralised sector's budgets and accounts are approved by the Comptroller General, which by its nature adopts a formal/legalistic approach. The Comptroller General does not carry out monitoring or evaluation of these institutions' spending and results to ensure that the money is spent efficiently on relevant programmes and achieves the declared objectives.

Finally, co-ordination mechanisms to ensure that the institutionally decentralised sector's objectives are in line with the government's objectives are weak. Officially, the Comptroller General supervises the execution of the institutionally decentralised sector's budgets, and measures results in terms of outcome; and both MIDEPLAN and the Comptroller General elaborate semi-annual and annual reports regarding compliance and progress of budget execution and performance. However, most of the institutionally decentralised sector's resources come from funding schemes which are largely independent from the national budget process, and as these institutions are autonomous, they do not discuss their objectives or performance with the government nor the Comptroller General. Therefore, the government lacks effective instruments and mechanisms to ensure that the objectives of the institutionally decentralised sector institutions are in line with the National Development Plan.

## *Insufficient co-ordination of capital budgeting across public institutions*

Most capital expenditure in Costa Rica is carried out by non-financial and financial public institutions (2.1% and 0.7% of GDP respectively), which are not accounted for as government in OECD National Accounts. General government (i.e. excluding financial and non-financial public enterprises) capital spending in Costa Rica represents only 2.5% of GDP. This is low both in comparison to OECD and to other LAC countries. Within the capital expenditure of general government, deconcentrated bodies represent 46% and decentralised non-business institutions another 20%. Central government (national budget) is responsible for only 25% of total general government expenditure and its rate of execution is very low (around 55%). Local governments (whose budgets are approved by the Comptroller) account for an additional 9% (information provided by Ministry of Finance).

According to the *Recommendation of the Council on Budgetary Governance* (Principle 3), the capital budgeting framework should be designed to meet national development needs in a cost-effective and coherent manner. But in Costa Rica, the multiplicity of budgets and lack of co-ordination mechanisms also has consequences on public investment. As mentioned previously, the institutionally decentralised public sector institutions are not subject to performance agreements or controls, and are free to allocate their budget to their own priorities. In principle, their investments must be aligned with the National Development Plan, but in practice there is no enforcement mechanism, and no instrument to control whether this is indeed the case.

## Recommendations

The challenges described in the previous section have two main consequences. First, in order to finance new government priorities, Costa Rica runs significant budget deficits, which threaten fiscal sustainability. Second, the government has very little control over the allocation and performance of general government and total public spending, so it is necessary to find a mechanism to monitor the institutionally decentralised public institutions and make sure their plans are coherent with the National Development Plan.

Given the limited capacity of the government to reallocate funds from one spending area to another, it is all the more important to improve the efficiency and effectiveness of the use of funds within each spending area, and to reallocate funds from one programme to another within the mandated spending floors. It would also be important to create a mechanism to ensure that the institutionally decentralised institutions' actions are in line with the government plan.

While budget rigidities constrain budget decisions, there is room to improve spending efficiency and prioritisation within the mandated expenditure. This section presents some policy recommendations to address the issues identified above.

### *Creating and ensuring fiscal space for government priority spending*

Budget earmarks are enshrined in the law, and some even in the Constitution. Eliminating or reducing budget rigidities would therefore require legal and/or constitutional changes. However, alternative mechanisms could be developed to effectively protect those areas which constitute national priorities. For example, some important allocations could be based on formulas, but these would have to be based on needs and population, rather than on revenues or GDP. Specific studies could be carried out to determine the most efficient way to protect spending in priority areas, as a basis to prepare and discuss a reform of budget earmarks in the Legislative Assembly.

The national planning could be transformed from a process-driven mechanism into a modern, government-wide strategy for delivering clear goals and objectives. Given the importance of the institutionally decentralised institutions in public spending, these should also be included in this process. The elements of such a development, which should be shaped by, and driven from, the centre of government, would include: 1) each sector leader (i.e. minister) or decentralised institution manager setting down a small number of measurable medium-term objectives at the start of each government term; 2) empowering this minister to allocate resources within that sector domain to achieve these results, and to reallocate resources from year to year as priorities evolve and to take account of objective evaluation results – even where this involves adjusting the resources available to institutionally decentralised institutions; 3) each minister/manager giving a public account of progress each year to the national assembly.

Spending reviews (Box 4.5) could be useful to identify options for reductions to baseline spending and to reallocate spending. Allowing ministries to keep the identified savings and allocate them to new priorities is a good incentive to ensure their co-operation in the identification of possible savings.

Pay-as-you-go rules try to correct this by conditioning the allocation of resources to new programmes to the termination or reduction of others by a similar amount. In theory, this would not only keep a sector portfolio reasonably stable, but should also ensure productivity gains. Indeed, to be justified, new programmes should deliver more value for money than those that are being phased out. The main risk of this approach is political arbitrage, since government programmes are not always valued for their contribution to social well-being but by their political impact. Thus, oftentimes, ministries propose cutting a programme with the knowledge that they will be reinstated under (political) pressure. Costa Rica could apply this type of pay-as-you-go rule, to give incentives to line ministers to find savings within their existing programmes, in order to finance new government priorities within the existing budget envelope. Spending reviews could be used to find these potential savings.

Costa Rica could envisage setting a time limit to new programmes and/or legislation mandating them. Even if programmes are judged as a priority and necessary, such limit – or sunset – gives an opportunity to revisit their justification, rationale and performance against expected results (Marcel, 2014). The results of such an assessment may lead to the termination of the programme, redesign or extension, depending on the findings and recommendations. The important feature of this approach is that it brings the assessment of the performance of a programme back to those that introduced it, making it easier to judge it on the basis of the reasons that justified its creation in the first place. Of course, this could generate some degree of uncertainty among administrators and beneficiaries, which can be reduced by carrying out evaluations sufficiently ahead of the sunset date.

### Box 4.5. Conceptual framework for spending reviews

Spending review is the process of developing and adopting savings measures based on the systematic scrutiny of baseline expenditure.

Spending reviews may be efficiency reviews (focused on savings through improved efficiency) and/or strategic reviews (focused on savings achieved by reducing services or transfer payments).

There are four stages in the spending review process: the framework stage (deciding the key design features of the spending review system); the parameters stage (deciding specific savings targets, review topics, procedural calendar, etc.); the savings option stage (developing savings options to be put forward to the final decision makers); and finally the savings decision stage (the final decisions on which savings measures will be implemented).

During the savings options stage, there are three alternative approaches which may be taken in assigning roles to the Ministry of Finance and spending ministries: bottom-up review (spending ministries develop their own savings options, with alternatives prepared by the Ministry of Finance); joint review (savings options are developed in a joint spending ministry/Ministry of Finance review teams); and top-down review (savings options are developed by the Ministry of Finance with limited spending ministry involvement).

Spending reviews examine review topics, which may be of three types: programme reviews (which seek to identify strategic and/or efficiency savings in specific programmes); process reviews (focused on business processes); and agency reviews (which review whole ministries or other agencies). A horizontal review focuses on the review topic which cuts across several government agencies (e.g. a review of government-wide procurement practices).

Selective spending review is spending review which focuses on a specific list of review topics which are decided at the outset (i.e. during the parameters stage) of the spending review

**Box 4.5. Conceptual framework for spending reviews** *(cont.)*

process. By contrast, comprehensive spending review is not constrained by any such *ex ante* list of review topics, and aims to review spending in greater depth. Comprehensive spending review does not literally try to examine everything.

*Source*: Robinson, M. (2014), "Spending reviews", *OECD Journal on Budgeting*, Vol. 13/2, OECD Publishing, Paris, http://dx.doi.org/10.1787/budget-13-5jz14bz8p2hd.

Costa Rica could reinforce performance-informed budgeting practices, with clear outputs that can be used as a basis for organisational accountability. This output-based approach should also be applied to the decentralised public sector. Performance budgeting allows countries to systematically incorporate performance data into the budget process. The implementation of performance budgeting requires adopting financial management information systems that facilitate the collection of performance data, adjusting the budget process to incorporate the information into budget allocations, establishing appropriate incentives at the management level and developing institutional capacity to carry out the process. Such performance-informed budgeting could be complemented with periodical evaluations. The main advantage of evaluations over performance indicators is that evaluations can lead to some clearer judgements on the justification, effectiveness and impact of government programmes.

### *Aligning decentralised institutions with government priorities*

While changing the governance structure of existing institutions is challenging, it is important to design efficient accountability, monitoring and evaluation mechanisms for future institutionally decentralised institutions. A checklist of issues the government should address when creating a new agency, based on the experience of OECD Members, could be helpful: 1) is an agency the best way of carrying out this public policy/public service; 2) does the agency need to be autonomous; 3) does the agency need to have legal personality; 4) what control mechanisms are in place in the statutes of the new institution (including performance indicators, with a process for updating these), in particular, agree on performance indicators for monitoring its activity since the creation, and design a process for regular updating of these indicators; 5) integration in the agency's statutes of sunset clauses or periodic evaluations of the need to renew the mandate of the agency, reform it or close it.

The government could envisage assessing the alignment of the existing institutionally decentralised sector with government priorities by addressing the following elements: 1) how does the institution help in meeting national development goals; 2) is the institution (still) needed to meet government priorities; 3) is the institution (still) the best way to deliver these services/goods; 4) is the institution efficient in doing so. Such a large-scale revision would face several challenges. First, should the different types of decentralised institutions be treated differently? Second, such an exercise would need to have a strong mandate from an institution with the power to impose it on the reviewed agencies. Third, what would be the best institution to carry out the assessment? And fourth, what should be done with the results?

Transfer payments represent about 30% of central government spending, in particular to finance decentralised institutions. In most OECD Members, such transfers come with conditionality, about how they will be spent and the outcomes to be achieved. Costa Rica could envisage reviewing all the transfers from the central government to the decentralised institutions, the objectives to be achieved with these funds, and agree with the decentralised institutions on performance targets to be used for evaluating whether these targets have been met.

Co-ordinating different actors with different strategic objectives is a challenging task. Experience shows that the higher the political level of the institution responsible for co-ordination, the more effective it is. In addition, the higher the level of the representatives of the different stakeholders in the co-ordination body, the more decision-making power they have to take decisions. If such an institution was created, it should therefore be placed in a high-ranking institution and the decentralised institutions should be represented by the general manager.

### *Ensuring fiscal sustainability*

Costa Rica could recommit to fiscal discipline by reactivating its well-designed constitutional requirements that have no legal reality at present. This could take the form of a fiscal responsibility law, in the light of modern experience with fiscal rules. Fiscal rules typically cover revenue, expenditure, budget balance or debt. They are meant to be observable and permanent, irrespective of changes in government. By restricting the degree of discretionary spending, fiscal rules help ensure consolidation efforts are respected in the short term, leading to a more sustainable fiscal position in the medium term. Furthermore, fiscal rules help governments signal their commitment to strengthening the institutional basis of fiscal responsibility laws. There is no one-size-fits-all approach for fiscal rules as the specific economic, political and social factors that influence fiscal policy in each country must be considered. Steps to be taken include determining the appropriate type of rule, the objective of the rule, its anti-cyclical capacity and escape clauses and adjusting budget procedures to align them with the fiscal rule.

It would be helpful for the Ministry of Finance to set out at the start of each government term a comprehensive medium-term fiscal framework. Such a medium-term fiscal framework would show the totality of aggregate revenues and expenditures forecast to arise over the four-year period of government, and would thus show how fiscal discipline would be ensured, in the light of the fiscal responsibility law. Such a medium-term fiscal framework could be complemented with a medium-term expenditure framework (showing the resources to be allocated to each of the key sector areas). Such a framework is useful to give some indication and assurance to sector leaders about the resources at their disposal to achieve key planning objectives. For such a medium-term fiscal framework and medium term expenditure framework to be effective, Costa Rica should adopt top-down budget practices. Typically in top-down budgeting, the executive first determines aggregate public finance targets (spending and revenue levels) given medium-term fiscal objectives and prevailing economic conditions. Within this aggregate, sectoral ceilings are set (and approved by Cabinet) reflecting existing commitments, political priorities in general and key new policy initiatives. The detailed allocation decisions are typically delegated to individual line ministries.

Costa Rica could envisage creating an independent fiscal institution or assigning that role to an already existing independent institution. An effective, medium-term fiscal framework must not only rely on credible, independent macroeconomic estimations (currently provided by the Central Bank), but has to be complemented by an important role in monitoring the compliance and implementation of fiscal rules. The capacities required are those needed to carry out economic and fiscal projections (with a short- to medium-term horizon, or long-term scenarios); baseline projections (assuming unchanged policies); analysis of the executive's budget proposals; monitoring compliance with fiscal rules or official targets; costing of major legislative proposals; and analytical studies on selected issues.

Costa Rica could adopt tools and procedural rules that can make the fiscal examination of permanent legislation more rigorous, in order ensure that the long-term fiscal cost of legislation is correctly understood and taken into account by the Legislative Assembly when voting it. The evaluation of the long-term expenditure impact of proposed legislations is a task which could be entrusted to an independent fiscal institution.

A single centrally controlled treasury fund for all public revenues and expenditure – including decentralised institutions – could be worth considering. Today, some decentralised institutions are running surpluses and accumulating reserves while the central government runs deficits and needs to issue debt. Revenue sources of the decentralised institutions (in particular, central government transfers) should be reviewed, to ensure that they are coherent with the resources needed by these institutions to carry out their tasks.

## Notes

1. Ministry of Finance, STAP, Analysis and Fiscal Monitoring Unit, consolidated by institutional classification, general government.

2. OECD National Accounts provide information by central government, state, local and social security. Many OECD Members also have autonomous and semi-autonomous institutions, and all their transactions must be reclassified into these categories, according to the institution to which these are related. In Costa Rica, deconcentrated bodies (*organos desconcentrados*) would be classified into central government. A large share of the decentralised non-business institutions corresponds to the Costa Rican Department of Social Security and would be classified as social security. Another important share of this corresponds to the five state universities, which would be classified in central government. The remaining elements would have to be reclassified into central government or local government on a case-by-case basis.

3. In OECD Members, central government includes autonomous and semi-autonomous institutions which are not computed in the number for Costa Rica. If these were not counted, the average number for OECD Members would be lower.

# *References*


Marcel, M. (2014), "Budgeting for fiscal space and government performance beyond the great recession", *OECD Journal on Budgeting*, Vol. 2013/2, OECD Publishing, Paris, http://dx.doi.org/10.1787/budget-13-5jz2jw9t0pd3.

Ministry of Finance (2013), "Marco fiscal presupuestario de mediano plazo, 2013-2018" ("Medium-term fiscal framework, 2013-2018"), Dirección General de Presupuesto, San José, www.hacienda.go.cr/docs/52224ab8cd313_MARCO%20PRESUPUESTARIO%20MEDIANO%20PLAZO%202013_2018.pdf.

OECD (2015), *Recommendation of the Council on Budgetary Governance*, OECD, Paris, http://acts.oecd.org/Instruments/ShowInstrumentView.aspx?InstrumentID=319&InstrumentPID=347&Lang=en&Book=False.

OECD (2014a), *Building on Basics, Value for Money in Government*, OECD Publishing, Paris, http://dx.doi.org/10.1787/9789264235052-en.

OECD (2014b), *Budgeting Practices and Procedures in OECD Countries*, OECD Publishing, Paris, http://dx.doi.org/10.1787/9789264059696-en.

OECD (2013), *Colombia: Implementing Good Governance*, OECD Public Governance Reviews, OECD Publishing, Paris, http://dx.doi.org/10.1787/9789264202177-en.

OECD/IDB (2014), *Government at a Glance: Latin America and the Caribbean 2014: Towards Innovative Public Financial Management*, OECD Publishing, Paris, http://dx.doi.org/10.1787/9789264209480-en.

Republic of Costa Rica (1949), *Constitución Política de la República de Costa Rica*, www.constitution.org/cons/costaric.htm.

Robinson, M. (2014), "Spending reviews", *OECD Journal on Budgeting*, Vol. 13/2, OECD Publishing, Paris, http://dx.doi.org/10.1787/budget-13-5jz14bz8p2hd.

# Chapter 5.

# Supporting human resources management in Costa Rica

*This chapter examines the strengths and weaknesses of the human resources management policies and practices of Costa Rica's Civil Service Regime. It formulates recommendations in five key reform areas: timely and accurate workforce data; the development of a merit-based, transparent and financially sustainable compensation system; the introduction of a coherent competency framework; an enhanced performance management system; and the development of institutional and individual leadership. The chapter highlights the importance of these reforms to promote better governance and improved public service design and delivery.*

## Public employment: The institutional set-up

Costa Rica's public governance stands out in the region, due in no small part to the country's professionalised civil service underpinned by a commitment to merit-based public employment. Costa Rica consistently ranks highest in the region on civil service development indicators. Today, however, the country is facing a new set of modern challenges and is rightly questioning whether the workforce management arrangements it had established to guide progress in the years past are those that will continue to ensure progress and prosperity in the years to come.

The structure of public employment is divided into a number of administrative divisions. The Constitution of 1949[1] and the subsequent Civil Service Statue of 1953[2] established the Civil Service Regime (CSR) to regulate public employment in the national executive branch, which includes ministries and their subsidiary bodies – a total of 47 entities covering about one-third of public employees, including teachers, who make up approximately 70% of this group. The Civil Service Directorate General (CSDG) acts as the central co-ordinating agency for public employment and human resources management (HRM) policies for the 47 entities of the CSR.[3] Within and across these 47 entities, there is a relatively consistent employment framework, with a common pay scale,[4] job classification, and terms and conditions of employment.

Outside the CSR, most public institutions have their own legislation regulating public employment and HRM practices. In addition, collective agreements in various institutions give employees privileges regarding pay, bonuses, incentives and working hours, which vary from one institution to the next. This myriad legislation and collective agreements lead to a plurality of HRM systems and policies, which results in significant disparity in the treatment of employees across institutions. The "decentralised public sector" (outside of the CSR) tends to offer better salaries and benefits, with greater employment flexibility.

Many institutions outside the CSR still fall under the scope of the Budgetary Authority. The Budgetary Authority establishes and monitors the number of employees for each institution under its scope and determines payment policies according to guidelines issued by the President and the Ministry of Finance. Approximately 58% of the entities under the scope of the Budgetary Authority belong to the CSR; an additional 29% use the same pay scale and job classification system as the CSR but do not fall within the CSR, and the remaining 13% have their own pay scale. The scope of the Budgetary Authority does not include municipalities, state universities, the Costa Rican social security institution, the legislative and judicial branches, the electoral tribunal institutions, nor auxiliary bodies to the legislative authority such as the Ombudsman, Auditor General and various public corporations such as the telecommunications and power authority (*Instituto Costarricense de Electricidad*, ICE) and the postal service.

The 2015-18 National Development Plan includes public employment as a priority and recognises the role of effective human resources management to strengthen the public institutions of the Costa Rican government. To implement the priorities of the plan, the government is considering the creation of public employment status categories that support standardised principles and transverse objectives, but at the same time recognise and respect the special needs and characteristics of each sector and institution. This would be a guided by a National Employment Policy.

## Improving data as a foundation of effective and strategic human resources management

Timely and accurate workforce data is essential to effectively manage, plan and control the size, costs and organisation of the workforce. Without basic information, the government of Costa Rica will be challenged to take informed decisions on how best to deploy the workforce to meet its goals and objectives. Without good management information, strategic workforce management is severely constrained. It should include factors such as level of education, skills and competencies, in order to best align particular capacities with the right priorities. It should also consider factors that impact cost, such as age and rank, and years of service.

In Costa Rica, it is difficult to get an exact picture of the structure of public employment and the number and distribution of public employees, as there is no central database to collect employee statistics in the CSR or beyond. A 2013 assessment of HR capacity in CSR organisations (CSDG, 2013) indicates a lack of capacity to maintain useful workforce data in most institutions. The workforce information management practices of several OECD Members like Belgium, Canada or the United Kingdom, which carry out whole-of-government assessment and analysis of the government workforce, may be of interest to Costa Rica. Costa Rica may also wish to look at a number of individual ministries' practices and consider the possibility of extending those that work well to other institutions. The Ministry of Health's HR information system may be worth studying in this regard.

Improving the quality and consistency of workforce data in Costa Rica should be seen as a fundamental step improving the transparency of the sector and enabling more informed HRM decision making. When linked to salary information, it will also help to better manage and control the costs of the workforce, an important challenge Costa Rica is facing.

## Towards a more merit-based, transparent and sustainable compensation system

Costa Rica's commitment to merit-based hiring practices and a professionalised civil service have set it apart from neighbouring countries; however, the merit principle could be strengthened by ensuring that employees' compensation is based on the nature of their work and the competencies they bring to it. Currently the Costa Rican salary system is very difficult to control, adjust, target and manage, due in part to the lack of an integrated database on public employment, no fiscal ceiling that limits the pay envelope, complex combinations of bonuses and allowances that differ greatly from employee to employee, and an interrelated web of collective agreements and legislation that tie increases in salary of one group to another.

Pay determination in Costa Rica is a complex affair. For many of the more senior positions, base salary only accounts for as little as 20% of total pay. The system of "pluses", bonuses and allowances added to base pay enables organisations to raise pay through means that are less transparent and controllable. While the majority of decentralised institutions follow the CSR's job classification and base salary standards, there is no common standard for pluses and bonuses. Hence, it is easy to maintain disequilibrium through the use of such tools while still maintaining compliance with the overall framework.

The complexity of this system leads to a variety of pay distortions which diverge from the merit principle of equal pay for equal work. The misalignment of pay to the value of work can have a demotivating impact on the workforce, particularly for those who perceive their work as less valued by their organisation. These imbalances can also have a direct impact on the capacity of organisations to attract and retain the right employees. The youngest and brightest graduates are more easily attracted by organisations willing to pay more, and the CSR cannot compete. Furthermore, there is anecdotal evidence of CSR institutions investing in staff development only to have high-performing staff leave for better paying jobs in richer decentralised agencies. While a certain level of mobility between organisations can have a positive impact on the workforce, this kind of predatory staffing can result in capacity imbalances that are not driven by strategic objectives.

Costa Rica could simplify the system by beginning a slow transition towards a "single salary" system, meaning an amalgamation of base salary and pluses. Any additional payments on top of base salary need to be universal and made as transparent and simple as possible. This does not need to initially result in a reduction of salary for any staff, and given the legal constraints, it may only be possible to implement this policy for new employees. This means taking a long-term view (up to 35 years) and therefore increases the urgency to begin. The national bank and the Auditor General's Office (Box 5.1) have already begun, and can provide models.

Controlling salary costs does not necessarily require a unified pay framework across all public sector organisations. In fact, completely uniform public employment and salary systems covering the entire public sector is not a common feature in OECD Members. All OECD Members struggle to balance salary coherence with organisational discretion to adjust salaries to meet their particular circumstances. They solve this tension differently, based on their unique administrative, political and constitutional contexts. Belgium and France, for example, use uniform salary legislation combined with adaptation in secondary legislation which enables adjustments to specific groups as required. Some OECD Members – such as Denmark, Finland, New Zealand and Sweden – have replaced traditional civil service systems with an extensive decentralisation of actual salary setting and enforced employer co-ordination linked to bargaining processes and collective agreements. These countries have also developed mechanisms for supporting and monitoring decentralised salary setting. These include supporting budgeting arrangements, guidelines and salary statistics.

The complexity of the pay system, the range of actors involved and the highly sensitive nature of the topic create a difficult working environment for reformers and can lead to a sense of paralysis. The approach of the national public employment policy would be to centralise control of pay under one authority for the entire public sector. While this may produce results in Costa Rica, this is not the direction that most OECD Members are moving towards. Costa Rica may wish to consider alternate approaches that link pay reform to broader budget reforms. This, however, would depend upon the development of more strategic HRM frameworks which would emphasise competency-based management, performance management and professional public sector leadership. These are taken up in the following sections.

## Competency management as foundation for a more strategic human resources management in the Civil Service Regime

An integrated and coherent competency framework could help to guide strategic HRM in the CSR or beyond. This section will discuss how the development of such a framework could enable more effective and coherent workforce planning, recruitment and selection, mobility and employee development within and across CSR organisations.

### Box 5.1. The implementation of a single salary scale scheme: The case of the Central Bank and the Comptroller General

As an effort to contain and gradually revert the profound disparities that pluses and annuities had created on their system of remunerations, the Central Bank and the Comptroller General implemented a single scale salary scheme for their employees. Below are some of the objectives behind such initiatives:

- to produce an employment system that attracts and retains talent
- to guarantee external competition by defining an objective percentile within which to place institutional salaries and be able to compare these against those in the National Financing Sector
- to ensure internal fairness, so that salary increases are proportional, or at least related to the level of responsibilities
- to have better instruments for training, classifying and evaluating staff.

In 1998, the Central Bank's Board of Directors approved the creation of a new salary scale that would be applied to all employees entering in 1999. Currently there are two wage scales operating: the single wage scale and the basic wage scale with pluses (depending on when the public servant started their career). The methodology includes: an inflation adjustment for two wage scales that function in parallel; an annual review of tendencies in the job market to adjust the global scale to those cases where salary is lower than those within the single scale; and finally, making adjustments on all wage salaries from changes resulting from inflation (i.e. reducing the loss of the salary's net worth against inflation). In the medium term, this approach has enabled the convergence of both scales, or at least has managed to close the wage breach between them. Currently, 60% of employees are employed under a global scale, so the challenge remains to eliminate the remaining disparities between employees in different wage scales.

The Office of the Comptroller General (Contraloría General de la República, CGR) implemented its single salary scheme in 2007 aiming for a unique wage scale amongst employees working in the head, management and administration offices. The single salary scale takes into account the annual wage and benefits under the Professional Career and Prohibition Regulation. Wage increases are implemented every two years in relation to cost of living and market adjustments. The CGR conducts studies of internal and external institutional wage imbalances. For external imbalances, a survey is conducted where internal salaries are compared to those of other institutions. On an institutional level, the wage objective for administrative and technical positions was set around the 40th and 60th percentiles, for professional positions between 60th and 80th percentiles, and for managerial and directive positions between the 80th and 95th percentiles. The CGR's unique salary scheme has been successful and transparent. About 40% of employees count with a unique salary. This reform has improved organisational climate, reduced costs and allowed for more merit-based recruitment processes.

*Source:* Information provided to the OECD by the Central Bank and the Comptroller General.

Costa Rica's CSR currently lacks effective workforce planning tools, and demonstrates various uneven levels of capacity in recruitment, mobility and workforce development. A recent assessment of HR capacity in 46 CSR organisations found that only the Ministry of Health and the Ministry of Finance have an active HR planning strategy and have incorporated competency management as part of their planning process (CSDG, 2013). This same report also found that most institutions are not able to evaluate candidates with regards to specific competencies needed to meet organisational goals. Almost half of the institutions report not having generated any mobility in the preceding two years. In terms of training and development, the assessment concluded that less than a quarter of institutions align their annual training plan to a long-term strategy based on organisational goals.

Using a common competency framework for planning, recruitment and selection, mobility and development could provide Costa Rica and the DGSC with a foundation to address the issues identified above, linking these processes under a common set of standards and understandings. A competency-based selection process enables organisations to better fill competency gaps identified in the workforce planning process while maintaining a high level of objective merit in the process. Competency management also supports horizontal and vertical mobility and agility by helping to define common career paths. Competency management also provides an effective and efficient way of aligning staff development investments with identified organisational requirements.

Costa Rica could build on its standard job classification system, which has recently been simplified, creating an excellent foundation to go the next step in identifying competencies that fit within each job class, across job categories and which are common for the entire organisation/CSR. There also appear to be pockets within the CSR where competency management has been developed which may be worth exploring to identify successful practices that could be adapted and spread more widely across the CSR. Institutions cited by the CSDG as having developed some level of competency management practices include: the Ministry of Health; Ministry of Finance; Ministry of the Economy, Industry and Trade; National Registry; and Ministry of Labour and Social Security. One path forward could be to engage key representatives from each of the organisations listed above to put together a multi-organisational task force to explore the idea of developing a CSR-wide competency framework. At the development stage, it would be ideal to keep the focus on the core CSR, with some participation of decentralised organisations if they are willing. Once a core set of competencies is developed and implemented in the CSR, other institutions may implement the same frameworks as they see the benefits stemming from the approach.

To be useful, competency frameworks should be oriented to future needs and organisational change, not to the past ways of structuring HR profiles. In a rapidly changing policy environment, competencies cannot be static. Whatever approach Costa Rica takes towards developing competency management, the country can learn a number of important lessons from the experience of OECD Members. Competency management can help to ensure that the civil service of Costa Rica has the range of skills needed to achieve the government's long-term goals. This suggests the need to consider how the work of the civil service is changing and which competencies the government requires to meet its long-term goals. OECD Members identify a range of future competencies needed for an agile, innovative public service. These have been clustered into the following four meta-competencies:

- creative thinking (creativity and innovation)
- strategic thinking (vision and future orientation)
- flexibility (flexibility and change management)
- co-operation (working collaboratively across boundaries and relationship building).

### Box 5.2. Competency management in the Belgian federal government

In the Belgian public services – both federal and regional – competencies are at the core of every HRM process, be it recruiting and selection, career management, performance appraisal and 360-degree feedback, knowledge management or the identification of critical functions. The greatest advantage of this approach is that competencies are linked to organisational needs – tactical or strategic – and that they provide a common language for all parties across the different services.

Competency management has been a central element since the launch of the Copernic Plan in 2000, focusing on a more integrated and strategic approach to HRM. It fundamentally changed recruitment and selection procedures, training and development, introducing workforce planning linked to organisational objectives.

The competency framework consists of:

- five key competencies that reflect the values of the federal government: service delivery orientation, team co-operation, loyalty, result orientation and self-development
- five groups of generic competencies considered necessary for all functions: information management, task management, management of employees, management of relationships and personnel management
- a large group of technical competencies which are specific to a type of work and supporting the profession itself.

A competency dictionary is available as a tool for HRM services, managers, chiefs and employees. There are 22 standard competency profiles, built around 3 roles: support, management and project management adapted to the employee level.

Implementing competency management resulted in some major recruitment system changes. The emphasis in entrance examinations shifted from testing knowledge to testing competencies. New procedures were put in place using a professional recruitment agency. Line managers and local HRM services are responsible for providing a job description and a competency profile for every recruit.[1]

Providing a comprehensive and clear-cut framework for managers is an ongoing priority in which the appropriate competencies are key as they determine the profile and remuneration of a manager. The framework depends on 12 generic competencies to which competencies specific to the position can be added. The competencies are:

- thinking (analysis; flexibility and innovation; vision and capacity for integration)
- human resources management (coaching, motivation and development of personnel; team management)
- interaction with the environment (collaboration and development of networks; orientation to citizens, internal clients and society)
- objectives (sense of responsibility; achievement of objectives; persuasion and negotiation)
- loyalty and integrity.

There is a strong link between competency management and performance appraisal as the annual evaluation scheme includes a discussion on the required competencies leading to (individual and team) development plans and training. Knowledge management is built around competencies, especially the technical competencies forming the heart of each function.

*Note:* 1. Online standard profiles are available at: www.federalecartografie.be/web/p1.php?z=z&lg=fr.

*Source:* OECD (2007), *OECD Reviews of Human Resource Management in Government: Belgium 2007: Brussels-Capital Region, Federal Government, Flemish Government, French Community, Walloon Region*, OECD Publishing, Paris, http://dx.doi.org/10.1787/9789264038202-en.

## Performance: Linking the investment in staff to better service outcomes

Performance management can play a vital role in linking the individual efforts of employees to larger organisational goals. It can also help to rationalise organisational structures and units by ensuring that each organisational sub-structure is capable of articulating its strategic goals in relation to those of the wider organisation, thereby enabling focus and clarity in mandate.

Within the CSR, the performance assessment system suffers from a high level of complexity and ratings inflation. The CSDG currently applies a performance rating scale for five "generic performance components" (service, efficiency, competency, flexibility and merit), where each organisation is asked to develop its own requirements and to rate each of these against a scale of 100 for individual employees. This is highly complex and moves away from the increasingly common OECD approach of simplifying ratings scales and using generic statements that are much easier for assessors and employees to understand. In order to work, the system needs to be simple enough that both the manager and employee understand what it means and how to use it. When a ratings scale is simple (e.g. 1-5), each score can be more easily understood. It also helps calibrate the scale so that the middle point of the scale is established as the norm. The upper levels should only be reserved for truly exceptional cases when employees have gone above and beyond the expectations of their employers and have, for example, worked extra time on a project beyond their job description or responded to shock or crisis in an exceptional way.

The CSDG and Ministry of National Planning and Economic Policy (*Ministerio de Planificación Nacional y Política Económica*, MIDEPLAN) are developing a pilot project to rethink the current performance assessment instruments, taking advantage of electronic databases and digital platforms currently under development to improve transparency and simplify the process. This is a promising opportunity to review OECD best practice in this area with a focus on simplifying the current guidelines and developing managers to implement the new programme. IT platforms can support performance assessment, providing a transparent mechanism to compile and share assessment information; however, the primary focus has to be first and foremost on developing an understandable tool that can be easily applied by managers and staff at all levels of the system with appropriate incentives for good performers. Pay for performance should not be an immediate priority. Instead, consideration should be given to improving the assessment instruments, training managers and staff to use them, and eventually linking them to career development and advancement. Finally, the CSR would benefit from a clear, transparent and fair policy for under-performers focused first on attempting to develop staff, with eventual dismissal for continued under-performance.

## Building institutional and individual leadership for a more coherent and effective Civil Service Regime

As one of its recent actions to modernise the CSR, the CSDG notes a move towards increased delegation of some HRM responsibilities to the HRM offices of the institutions under its authority. This is driven in part by limited budgetary resources in the CSDG as well as the desire to enable a more proactive and specialised HRM at the organisational level. The move towards increased delegation is also seen across many OECD Members. Central HRM authorities increasingly delegate HRM responsibilities to managers across the administration, providing them with guidance and support, as well as shared systems; however, the extent of HRM delegation varies among OECD Members. The trend towards delegating HRM responsibilities increases managerial flexibility, with the central HRM body taking a more strategic leadership role. However, it is important to note that delegation has happened to a greater extent in mature civil service systems in which core values are well-embedded and robust management accountability systems are in place. Experience in OECD Members shows that effective delegation of HRM authority has to be accompanied by:

- strengthening of the capacity of the central HRM body to monitor the implementation of HRM policy
- effective systems to hold managers accountable for their handling of delegated authority
- adequate managerial capacity and competence in ministries and other institutions.

Moving towards a delegated system in Costa Rica should not be primarily driven as a cost cutting exercise. While it is useful to recognise that the CSDG lacks the resources to manage all HRM across the CSR, delegation still requires a strong central HRM body, albeit a different set of competencies. It is also important to acknowledge that delegation can place significant strain on the HR offices of ministries and agencies, in particular in small organisations where the HRM capacity is limited. This could mean developing capacity in the CSDG to facilitate co-ordination, monitor, formulate policies and guidelines, and provide technical support to the individual institutions. In order to develop a stronger focus on these tasks, it could be worth assessing whether the current structure of the CSDG, which is primarily organised according to HRM sub-systems (e.g. salaries, recruitment, strategic development), prioritises the kind of responsibilities it needs to undertake and fully support delegated HRM.

Supporting ministries and agencies in an increasingly delegated environment also suggests the need to consider new tools and methods to support line ministries and agencies. There are a number of approaches that OECD Members use to enable this. These include: 1) fully delegating responsibility for some functions and monitoring them through management accountability frameworks; 2) simplifying centralised policy frameworks for more individualised implementation in the ministry; and 3) the use of communication tools and forums to ensure effective dialog and sharing of best practice experience.

Communication tools are also essential to develop a strong network of HRM professionals across the CSR who have the opportunity to exchange experience and input into policy development processes. The CSDG should ensure that it is using mechanisms such as its Human Resources Chief Management Assembly (where all 47 human resources chiefs are present), and the smaller Technical Advisory Council (made up of elected HR chiefs from the larger body) to their full potential. The focus should be on ensuring both two-way communication between the CSDG and institutions through information sharing and genuine consultation, as well as providing a forum for ministries and agencies to discuss and share experience amongst them.

Due to their strategic roles in government, there is an increased tendency among OECD Members to group senior civil servants separately and manage them under different HRM policies. While a great deal of variation exists across OECD Members in their approach to senior management, a number of trends exist. These include the development of specific management competencies which are applied to managers across all functions and support staffing processes for senior management positions.

### Box 5.3. Personnel Officers' Network in Ireland

**Function of the Personnel Officers' Network**

The key function of the Personnel Officers' Network (PON) is to provide a forum for personnel officers and HR managers in the civil service to discuss best practice human resources management procedures. The PON provides regular active networking opportunities which allows members to share their experience and address issues of mutual concern. In this way, the PON serves to identify and build upon administrative and policy initiatives, as well as develop and assist in the delivery of members' training needs, which improve HR management in the civil service.

The quarterly meetings of the PON comprise a mix of presentations and focused discussion regarding a variety of topics. They are structured in such a way that members have ample opportunity to network. The objectives of the meetings are:

- to discuss and develop best practice HRM in the civil service
- to agree cross-departmental approaches to implementation of HR processes
- to provide the opportunity for personnel officers to present their experiences and learn from each other
- to invite speakers to inform on strategic issues relating to HRM
- to provide feedback and ideas on the development and implementation of HR policies to the Department of Public Expenditure and Reform.

An electronic workspace has been provided for the network and is used for discussions, sharing of ideas and initiatives. This workspace stores presentations and meeting agendas, records membership and contact details, provides opportunities to engage on work items, allows queries to be posted and contributed to, provides a facility for surveys and questionnaires, and ensures more productive formal meeting outputs and outcomes.

The Executive Committee is drawn from members of the network and must consist of at least eight members. Committee meetings are held prior to each meeting and as required to discuss and agree the agenda and future workplans. A quorum of five attendees is required for an Executive Committee meeting.

Secretarial support to the network is provided by the Civil Service Human Resources Directorate to assist with administrative and logistical arrangements.

There are sub-committees of the Personnel Officers' Network which meet and discuss topics as they arise. Such topics have included reform of sick leave, anti-bullying and harassment, and recruitment policies.

*Source:* Information provided to the OECD by Natasha Cray, Public Service Sick Leave Policy, Civil Service HR Division, Department of Public Expenditure and Reform, Ireland.

Costa Rica does not currently target training programmes towards managers or future managers. However, this is a new priority of the CSDG which has recently created a new division for management training. The emphasis of management development in Costa Rica should include both formal training to close gaps in leadership and management capabilities, and active learning methods to ensure managers' competencies remain up to date. The CSDG could take the lead on identifying priorities, setting the overall strategy of leadership development and designing the development framework. However, leadership and management development activities are most likely to be effective when they are defined as a high priority by the government, and could be guided by a task force of senior managers to ensure their buy-in from the beginning.

### Box 5.4. Chilean *Sistema de Alta Dirección Pública*

In 2003, the Chilean government, with the agreement of all political actors (opposition political parties, non-governmental organisations, civil society), created the *Sistema de Alta Dirección Pública* (ADP), a central senior civil service system. The aim of the ADP was to establish a professional senior management. Following the reform, there are three distinct groups:

- The most senior positions which are filled by direct designation by the government (1 000 positions out of 2 000 000 in central government).
- The ADP, for which recruitment is based on public competition (1 000 positions in central government). There are two levels within the ADP: approximately 1% at the first hierarchical level (heads of service, directors general), and the remainder at the second hierarchical level (regional directors, heads of division).
- Middle management positions (2 000 positions in central government) at the third hierarchical level, which form part of the career civil service.

The ADP system has been implemented gradually by recruiting by open competition whenever a post falls vacant and by expanding it over time to additional groups. For example, it has been expended to include 3 600 municipal education directors and 2 800 new senior management posts in municipalities.

Key features of the ADP are:

- competitive selection based on professional merit
- profile based on competencies which are evaluated by expert consultants
- three-year term of office, renewable for two subsequent terms
- right to severance pay
- assessment under management performance agreements
- possibility of removal by the President for poor performance or loss of confidence.

Most of the selection process for the ADP is contracted out to specialised recruitment agencies. The National Civil Service Directorate (DNSC) is responsible for management of the ADP. However, the Senior Public Management Council (*Consejo de Alta Dirección Pública*) is in charge of guaranteeing the transparency, confidentiality and absence of discrimination of the selection process. It is chaired by the director of the DNSC and has four members proposed by the President of Chile and approved by the Senate. The selection process, which takes about four months, begins with the publication of the vacancy notice in the media. A specialised enterprise commissioned by the Senior Public Management Council analyses the curricula vitae of the different candidates and prepares a shortlist for the council or a selection committee (under the council's supervision). Professional competence, integrity and probity are some of the criteria used in the selection process. Subsequently, the council or the committee selects the best candidates for interview and prepares a final shortlist for the competent authority for the final appointment.

The ADP system was based on international experience. In particular, the experience of OECD Members such as Australia and New Zealand strongly influenced the Chilean model. The system is considered one of the main achievements of the modernisation of Chile's public management. One effect has been the decline in the number of political appointees in the central government; they currently represent only 0.5% of the total public workforce. It is also argued that the presence of women in senior positions has increased under the system; they occupy 32% of positions, compared to 15% in the Chilean private sector.

*Source:* Weber, A. (2012), "Alta Dirección Pública", presentation given at the seminar Fortaleciendo la Capacidad del Empleo Público Colombiano, Bogota, 27 July.

## Implementing human resources management reforms for improved and sustained performance

One key lesson from OECD Members is that HRM reforms are more effective and stand a better chance of succeeding when they are based on an overall view of how government should function in order to meet emerging challenges. This means framing them in the context of a compelling vision of the future, based on an understanding of how the nature of public administration is changing and what kind of workforce Costa Rica needs to meet future challenges. It also means linking the design of HRM reforms to broader public administration initiatives and positioning HRM reforms as crucial supporters of these.

Costa Rica has begun the development of an integrated approach through the development of the sector-wide National Public Employment Policy (NPEP). The NPEP's ambition is commendable and, if implemented successfully, the plan may go a long way towards improving the coherence, efficiency and agility of the Costa Rica's public sector. It is a holistic approach driven by strategy. Its focus is on both the effectiveness of each individual sub-system as well as the connections between each. The NPEP could evolve towards a compelling and shared vision of the future that could help to bring together social partners and frame the dialog as a positive process of co-creation rather than beginning with current problems which lead too quickly to blame and protective reactions. Furthermore, rooting the HRM reforms in a larger programme of public administration modernisation would help to ensure effective co-ordination and visibility of HRM reforms.

It may be advisable for Costa Rica to give careful consideration to which venues and stakeholders should be involved in the future NPEP visioning and development process. In OECD Members, HRM reforms have often lagged behind because structural HR reforms tend to be politically sensitive and sometimes require difficult negotiations with unions. In order for the NPEP to be successful, it will require a high level of political will and support and must be dealt with as a political issue as much as a technical one. Costa Rica may wish to designate a strong minister to lead the reform at the Cabinet level, specific Cabinet committees to ensure broader buy-in and a similar structure at the administrative level. Organisational venues to support these structures should be fit for purpose – this may involve careful consideration of whether it would be useful to develop a new organisation for the oversight and implementation of reforms to give them more visibility and priority or whether existing organisations are adequate. Given the strength of unions in Costa Rica and their ability to block reforms at the Constitutional Court, reform success will also require early and genuine co-operation with the unions and other stakeholders. This role would likely need to be more than consultative to ensure genuine buy-in and long-term commitment.

The sequencing of a future NPEP implementation process is another factor that requires careful consideration. The NPEP is highly ambitious and commendable in its scope, but success will require skilled and committed leadership to implement effective change management as well as an engaged workforce which understands and supports the future vision. MIDEPLAN needs to carefully consider whether these preconditions are sufficiently established across the public sector and what can be done to build and develop these. A careful assessment of the current strengths and challenges in this regard may result in MIDEPLAN developing a more strategic sequencing of the implementation process in two respects: 1) choose a number of initial priority areas where quick wins can establish a positive reform experience to build upon; and 2) begin with improvements within the CSR and among other decentralised institutions whose missions, mandates and activities most closely align with and resemble those of the CSR, while leaving more autonomous institutions for possible incorporation at a later date.

## Recommendations

Costa Rica could use the collection and use of workforce data as a foundation of effective and strategic HRM. This could begin within the CSR and then be extended to additional agencies on an incremental basis. This should build on current effective approaches wherever possible to minimise additional burden to organisations.

Costa Rica could improve the merit focus of its compensation and improve control over workforce costs by first clarifying the interrelated webs of regulations and collective agreements to ensure a broad and consistent understanding of the existing situation among those responsible for the system. Next, the system could be simplified by incorporating existing pluses into a clear and simple base salary for new employees (the so-called single salary system). Finally, the salary envelope could be controlled through budgetary measures and controls.

Costa Rica could move towards more strategic management of its human resources by building on its job classification system to incorporate a competency framework and eventually integrating this into planning, recruiting/selection, mobility and development practices. A first step may involve engaging key representatives from each of the organisations listed above to put together a multi-organisational task force to explore the idea of developing a CSR-wide competency framework.

Costa Rica could improve performance management by simplifying and rethinking its performance assessment process for employees. Consideration should be given to improving the assessment ratings, training managers and staff to use them, and eventually linking them to career development and advancement. This would need to be accompanied by a clear, transparent and fair policy for under-performers focused first on attempting to develop staff, with eventual dismissal for continued under-performance.

Costa Rica could enhance the coherence of its CSR and beyond by focusing on institutional and individual leadership capacity. This could involve developing management accountability structures to ensure delegation is met with capacity and accountability at the agency level. Additionally, the Human Resources Chief Management Assembly and the Technical Advisory Council should be more leveraged to enable and support a strong HR community at the ministry level. Finally, Costa Rica could develop more strategic management of senior civil servants by designing a specific competency framework for this group and providing leadership training and development opportunities for senior managers and potential managers.

## Notes

1. Articles 191 and 192, Political Constitution of 7 November 1949.
2. Civil Service Statute, Law 1581 of 1953.
3. Article 7bis, Civil Service Statute, Law 1581 of 1953; and Article 4, Regulations of the Civil Service Statute, Executive Decree 21 of 1954.
4. MIDEPLAN (2012), "Estado de Situación en Materia de Salarios y Remuneraciones del Sector Público Costarricense", http://documentos.mideplan.go.cr/alfresco/d/d/workspace/SpacesStore/10db0638-c2b8-4bca-8816-2ef55367c4d1/Estado%20de%20situacion%20en%20materia%20de%20salarios%20y%20remuneraciones.pdf.

## *References*


CSDG (2013), "Diagnóstico de las Oficinas de Gestión Institucional de Recursos Humanos cubiertas por el Régimen de Servicio Civil de Costa Rica" ("Diagnosis of the Offices of Institutional Management of Human Resources Regime covered by the Civil Service Regime of Costa Rica"), document provided to the OECD by the Civil Service Directorate General.

OECD (2007), *OECD Reviews of Human Resource Management in Government: Belgium 2007: Brussels-Capital Region, Federal Government, Flemish Government, French Community, Walloon Region*, OECD Publishing, Paris, http://dx.doi.org/10.1787/9789264038202-en.

Weber, A. (2012), "Alta Dirección Pública", presentation given at the seminar Fortaleciendo la Capacidad del Empleo Público Colombiano, Bogota, 27 July.

# Chapter 6

# Supporting integrity policies in public procurement in Costa Rica

*This chapter studies reforms to the legal framework and the institutional set up to safeguard the integrity of the procurement process. The chapter examines the functions of the Comptroller General, the Ministry of Finance (Department of Management and Public Procurement) and of specialised units within each institution that are key actors in the procurement process. It also defines opportunities to strengthen the institutional framework as well as priority areas to increase integrity, transparency and accountability. The chapter gives recommendations on how the government of Costa Rica can use public procurement in a more transparent and effective manner to achieve policy objectives, i.e. by creating a public procurement authority or agreeing on a single procurement platform that covers the whole public sector, including the autonomous entities.*

## Public procurement in the Costa Rican economy

Public procurement is a key economic activity. It accounts on average for one-third of government spending in OECD Members. Its sound management is critical for a transparent and accountable spending of taxpayers' money and essential to build a stronger, cleaner and fairer global economy. Corruption and wrongdoing can have a profound impact on a country's capacity to maximise the use of available resources to provide high-quality services required by its citizens. Nowadays, governments need to provide public services with fewer resources, greater efficiency and ensure value for money due to budgetary constraints and greater demands for better services. Corruption in all its forms can arise in every phase of the procurement process, regardless of sector or scale. It is a threat to markets, trust in government and the rule of law; fighting corruption requires governments and business to work together.

Even though Costa Rica ranks better than other Latin American countries in Transparency International's Corruption Perception Index (CPI), the perception of corruption in Costa Rica has been increasing in the last few years. From 2010 to 2014, Costa Rica dropped 6 positions in the CPI. Levels of trust in government have also dropped, from 53% to 40% in the past five years, more than five times as much as the average decline across OECD Members for the same period (42.5% to 40%; Gallup World Poll, 2014). Corruption was further mentioned as one of the four most problematic factors for doing business in Costa Rica by the World Economic Forum's *Global Competitiveness Report 2014-2015.*

In Costa Rica, in 2014 general government public procurement accounted for approximately 15% of GDP (excluding oil revenues) and 30% of general government expenditure. For instance, procurement spending in Latin American and Caribbean (LAC) countries in 2011 represented 26% of general government expenditures and in 2013 OECD governments spent, on average, 29% of the total general government expenditure on public procurement. Despite public procurement's impact on the national budget, Costa Rica does not benefit from the strategic leverage of the procurement function as it is perceived as an administrative task. This activity does not fully achieve its strategic potential due to limited cohesive work from all institutions toward clear priorities and objectives and because public servants see this function primarily as an administrative checklist.

The major buyers in Costa Rica are autonomous institutions, especially the Costa Rican Electricity Institute (*Instituto Costarricense de Electricidad*, ICE), the National Road Council, the Costa Rican Department of Social Security (*Caja Costarricense de Seguro Social*, Caja), the Costa Rican Oil Refinery (*Refinadora Costarricense de Petróleo*, RECOPE) and the National Bank of Costa Rica. Overall, 92% of purchases are carried out by these autonomous institutions, 6% by the (budgetary) central government and about 2% by municipalities and other non-state entities (Banco Nacional de Costa Rica, 2010).

## The institutional anchorage and legal framework of public procurement

Costa Rica has a long-standing tradition of making efforts to achieve good management of public funds. These go back to 1825 (creation of Courts of Accounts by Congress), with additional milestones like the creation of the Comptroller's Office in 1950, supplemented with a sound legal framework.

The most important legislation regarding procurement is the Procurement Act, enacted in 1995 and covering most public institutions, defining amongst others the procurement plan and procurement procedures.[1] Other institutions, such as the ICE, have their own public procurement rules[2] and the *Caja* has special regulations on the procurement of medicines; differences include, for instance, shorter times for the different stages of the procurement process or different economic thresholds than other government agencies. For some of the institutions, these specific regulations are explained by the fact that these sectors are facing higher levels of competition and therefore demand greater flexibility and efficiency in their procurement processes. Other relevant legislation includes the Concession of Public Works General Act (Law 7762 of 1998).

The key actors in the procurement process in Costa Rica are the Comptroller General, the Ministry of Finance (Department of Property Management and Public Procurement, DPMPP), the Digital Government Technical Secretariat and specialised units within each institution. The DPMPP covers less than 20% of the public procurement spending, covering only 61 institutions (i.e. ministries and subsidiary bodies). The Comptroller General carries out three main functions: *ex ante* control (i.e. approval of budgets of territorially and institutionally decentralised institutions; but also for launching a public procurement procedure within almost all public entities and the approval of exceptions for public bidding), *ex post* control and bid protests resolution.

Recent reforms have been carried out at different levels, both for the legal framework and the institutional set-up. The Procurement Act underwent a review in 2006, which promoted the adoption of framework agreements. The Office of the Comptroller General (*Contraloría General de la República*, CGR) has been making efforts to reduce the amount of contracts under its approval, returning part of the responsibility to the procuring entity. In 2012, a reform was enacted to increase the economic threshold applicable to contracts subject to the CGR's review, in order to help the Procurement Division of the CGR focus primarily on highly complex procurement procedures (Comptroller General of the Republic, 2012). Several consecutive governments actively supported the implementation of digital government, showing a sustained strong political commitment to press forward with digital reform.

## Opportunities to strengthen the institutional framework

### *The need to fine-tune procurement-related functions*

The CGR's *ex ante* control function does not exist in the majority of supreme audit institutions (SAIs) in the OECD, while in the few where it is present, the scope is limited, either functionally (e.g. Italy) or financially (e.g. Portugal). The Lima Declaration indicates that *ex ante* control may be carried out by institutions other than SAIs or other audit institutions (INTOSAI, 1977). The Lima Declaration notes that *ex ante* audit has the advantage of being able to prevent damage to the state before it occurs but may create an excessive amount of work and overlap with other responsibilities. *Ex ante* control of legality – or *refrendo* as it is referred in Costa Rica – is a core element of the CGR's portfolio. *Refrendo* is a preventive, *ex ante* verification of the legality of certain administrative acts, exclusively focused on legal compliance *vis-à-vis* the whole spectrum of the national applicable legal framework. The *refrendo* is seen as an important control for the preservation of law and order that can be associated with legitimacy of administrative action and trust in government.

In addition to *ex ante* control, the CGR also carries out *ex post* control. In this respect, the CGR reviews how entities spent public funds and determines if they complied with the law. The CGR in Costa Rica, as in Brazil, Chile, Italy, Portugal and Spain, has the power to impose administrative sanctions to those responsible for committing illegal acts in the management of public funds and public patrimony. However, stakeholders mention that *ex post* controls are limited and the CGR should reinforce this role. Moreover, risks may arise by approving first and auditing later as well as approving the use of exceptions.

In many OECD Members there has been a general trend for the past 20 years to move away from *ex ante* audit assignments, where they have existed, towards *ex post* audit assignments and greater focus on the functioning of internal controls and performance (Ruffner and Sevilla, 2004). The move from *ex ante* to *ex post* audit in the public sector has been influenced by changes in the size of government, technological innovation, the shift towards performance management and new forms of service delivery (OECD, 2014a).

In recent years, there has been a move for SAIs to develop better awareness and understanding of the value and benefit that they provide for citizens (INTOSAI, 2010). The change from *ex ante* to *ex post* controls does not mean there is less control, but rather more varied types of control. This change places the burden on managers to implement effective internal control and risk management practices. However, the Lima Declaration points out that "the legal situation and the conditions and requirements of each country determine whether a supreme audit institution carries out pre-audit. Post-audit is an indispensable task of every supreme audit institution regardless of whether or not it also carries out pre-audits" (INTOSAI, 1977). Costa Rica could reassess the role of its CGR, within its constitutional mandate, reviewing the continued relevance of its existing assignments and exploring new ones. Costa Rica could start allowing entities to gradually reduce *ex ante* controls if entities can demonstrate improvements in internal control and risk management. The CGR will need to monitor and evaluate and if internal controls are deteriorated then the agency would once again be subject to *ex ante* control. The CGR can start to pilot this possibility on an entity or sector base.

The role of the CGR in guiding public sector internal audit is similar to OECD Members such as Denmark, Korea and Portugal. However, in Costa Rica there is no formal channel of communication between the different audit units that allow them to share similar experiences. Internal control verifies whether chains of responsibility are clear and the delegated levels of authority for approval of spending and sign-off, and approval of key procurement milestones are well-functioning (OECD, 2009). In strengthening the CGR's role in guiding internal audit, Costa Rica may, for instance, consider strengthening its internal audit support role through the creation of an online Portal for Internal Audit Units, like Chile, to support communications and share information with internal auditors in the central and municipal government.

Effective remedies for challenging procurement decisions are essential to build bidders' confidence in the integrity and fairness of the procurement system. Key aspects of an effective recourse system are timely access, independent review, efficient and timely resolution of complaints as well as adequate remedies (OECD, 2009). Providing remedies before the contested contract is signed is essential to make sure that an aggrieved bidder maintains a chance of winning the contract. The CGR in Costa Rica acts as the body where objections against tender documents can be filed by potential bidders and any legally established entity, looking after the interests of the community where the procurement takes places.

Furthermore, central purchasing bodies have been implemented in an increasing number of the OECD Members. They are embedded in the system of public administration of each country and reflect the specific structures for the provision of public services. A central purchasing body is a contracting authority that: 1) acquires goods or services intended for one or more contracting authorities; 2) awards public contracts for works, goods or services intended for one or more contracting authorities; or 3) concludes framework agreements for works, goods or services intended for one or more contracting authorities. Large procurement volumes could reduce prices by achieving economies of scale as well as increase competition. Furthermore, they reduce duplication and transaction costs, and increase certainty, simplicity and uniformity, allowing for more focused delivery of policy goals. Currently, in Costa Rica there is no centralised purchasing body or procurement authority with a strategic mandate to provide a cohesive procurement vision, guidelines, co-ordination and performance management of procurement. Most institutions have their own resources management, procurement vision and e-procurement platform. This limits a strategic and effective procurement function. The multiplicity of procurement bodies may further create some duplicity for both suppliers and entities and therefore lessen opportunities for creating economies of scale and lowering prices. According to the 2015 *OECD Recommendation of the Council on Public Procurement*, the procurement function should be governed by a co-ordinated procurement authority or unit with a unified and well-recognised strategic mandate. Central purchasing bodies can be state-owned enterprises as in 15.6% of OECD Members, or function as a government agency (43.8%) or operate under a line ministry (28.1%). In this sense, in Costa Rica, the DPMPP could have its role strengthened and carry out this function.

### Box 6.1. **Online Portal for Internal Audit Units in Chile**

In 2012, the Chilean CGR created an online Portal for Internal Audit Units (*Portal para las Unidades de Auditoría o Control Interno*) in order to support communications and share information with internal auditors in the central and municipal governments.

The portal serves both as a means of CGR communication and information sharing and also a means for discussion and knowledge sharing among internal auditors.

For example, the portal makes available CGR news, determinations, court of accounts' decisions regarding the actions of internal auditors, frequently used norms, accounting norms, INTOSAI norms, documents of interest and a directory of approximately 1 000 government internal auditors.

In addition, the portal includes a discussion forum structured around four themes:

1. matters spanning across levels of government
2. matters related to the central government sector (i.e. ministries, agencies and public enterprises)
3. matters related to the municipal sector
4. matters related to public sector accounting

*Source:* OECD (2014a), *Chile's Supreme Audit Institution: Enhancing Strategic Agility and Public Trust*, OECD Public Governance Reviews, OECD Publishing, Paris, http://dx.doi.org/10.1787/9789264207561-en.

### *Recommendations*

Costa Rica could create a public procurement authority, within the limits of the Constitution, to set a national procurement vision, procurement priorities and objectives, including savings and policy objectives. This public procurement authority could also consolidate goods and services and promote a more expansive use of framework agreements. Costa Rica could undertake an awareness campaign to establish trust and confidence among the different actors on the benefits of a procurement authority as done by the Portuguese National Agency for Public Procurement (ANCP).

**Box 6.2. Launching an awareness campaign in Portugal**

The Portuguese National Agency for Public Procurement (ANCP) launched an awareness-raising campaign when it was established in 2007, consisting in:

- A road show with meetings in all large Portuguese cities for civil servants and bidders and open to all. Contacts through universities, technical chambers, chambers of commerce were sought and used.
- Direct information sessions for buyers, in particular big or strategic buyers.
- A large and advertised public conference and launching event with political participation, in two parts: the first part with the participation of national political leaders, and the second part with international organisations and similar international authorities.

The ANCP is now a well-known authority which sets up framework agreements and provides procurement advice: its role is recognised country-wide. The ANCP was merged with the ESPAP in September 2012 and now the ESPAP is in charge of public procurement activities for the Portuguese government.

*Source:* OECD (2014b), *Spain: From Administrative Reform to Continuous Improvement*, OECD Public Governance Reviews, OECD Publishing, Paris, http://dx.doi.org/10.1787/9789264210592-en.

Costa Rica could start allowing entities to gradually reduce *ex ante* controls if entities can demonstrate improvements in internal control and risk management. The CGR will need to monitor and evaluate the quality of internal controls. The CGR can start to pilot this possibility on an entity or sector base. The CGR could, in addition, facilitate a communication network amongst internal control units. This implies a reassessment of the role of its Comptroller General, within its constitutional mandate, implying a review of the continued relevance of its existing assignments and exploration of new ones.

## Opportunities to promote transparency and accountability in public procurement

### *Priority areas to increase transparency and accountability*

The Costa Rican procurement system is substantially fragmented. In 2001, the Ministry of Finance launched Compr@Red, a digital platform for procurement procedures in the central government which covers today 61 institutions. In 2009, the Digital Government Technical Secretariat developed a further e-procurement system known as Mer-Link, covering several autonomous entities and municipalities, including the biggest buyer, the ICE. Moreover, some institutions, such as the *Caja*, the Costa Rican Oil Refinery, the National Insurance Institute and the National Training Institute, have developed their own procurement platforms. This diversification of procurement platforms can have different disadvantages. It results, among others, in elevated human and financial resources needed for operating the different systems, higher costs for suppliers as well as non-standardised tender documents and bidding processes (and guidelines and manuals follow processes in their diversity). At the beginning of 2015, Executive Decree 38830-H-MICITT mandated that Mer-Link and Compr@Red be merged into a single e-procurement system named SICOP (*Sistema Costarricense de Compras Públicas*). The new platform will be primarily Mer-link but some of Compr@Red's functionalities will be merged into Mer-link. However, the decree does not make the system mandatory for the autonomous institutions, which could contribute in the future to the same proliferation of platforms that exists today in Costa Rica, limiting the benefits of a single platform. In addition, even if initially the Ministry of Finance will cover the cost that entities will have to pay to use SICOP, at some point entities will have to pay to use the system. Fees need to be clearly defined and agreed on before the full implementation of the system to ensure it is properly implemented. To take full advantage of the e-system, proper training needs to be provided to procurement agents, potential bidders and suppliers, as low knowledge and skills of ICT has been identified as the main challenges to use e-procurement systems.

Costa Rica's procurement units are used to having different thresholds to carry out their procurement procedures, whereas this can create confusion and extra work for suppliers as well as have an impact on the negotiation power of the ministries or small institutions *vis-à-vis* powerful autonomous institutions. The threshold to carry out different procedures differs among institutions related to the allocated budget: the higher the budget, the higher the threshold to carry out the direct awards. Most OECD Members have a single set of thresholds, without taking into consideration the size of the budget of each procuring entity.

Contrary to most OECD Members, where public bidding is the procurement procedure used the most, in Costa Rica during 2013, 82% in terms of number and 40% in term of value of the procedures were awarded through limited tendering. In addition, 41% of the procedures in terms of value were awarded through selective tendering. It is worth mentioning that limited tendering and selective tendering in Costa Rica are open and competitive processes similar to public biddings but with simplified procedures and shorter deadlines. All potential suppliers registered in the platforms are invited to participate in the process and submit proposals. Notwithstanding, the excessive use of these modalities may reflect an attempt to avoid more complex, and longer, tendering processes that have more requirements and formalities and are perceived by procurement officials as burdens, or may result from a lack of planning at the level of both requirement forecasting and management of the procurement process.

In recent years, the DPMPP has promoted the adoption of framework agreements, following a reform to the Procurement Act in 2006.[3] Frameworks agreements are applicable to the 61 entities under the DPMPP.[4] Framework agreements currently in force cover, among others, the purchase of office supplies and stationary, cleaning services and airline tickets. This has allowed, among other things, to consolidate demand and therefore reduce prices by achieving economies of scale, increase the negotiation power *vis-à-vis* powerful institutions, reduce the interaction between procurement agents and the private sector, and increase efficiency, since each ministry can place its purchase orders through the e-procurement platform Compr@Red.

Procurement officials in Costa Rica adopt a compliance-based approach rather than a more strategic approach based on outcomes as there is no professionalised procurement workforce. There is no special recruitment process for procurement units. Procurement units are staffed in relation to the size of the institution and the complexity of its procedures, and they include public administration professionals, lawyers, economists and industrial engineers, among others. Across OECD Members, public procurement is increasingly recognised as a strategic profession rather than a simple administrative function that plays a central role in preventing mismanagement, waste and potential corruption.[5] Adequate public employment conditions and incentives – in terms of remuneration, bonuses, career prospects and personnel development – help attract and retain highly skilled professionals. Many countries have started applying national integrity standards for all public officials – for example in civil service regulations – and standards for specific at-risk positions, such as for procurement officials, tax and customs officials or financial authorities. Specific standards for procurement officials, such as codes of conduct and conflict of interest policies, mitigate the risks related to the specificities of the public procurement process as done by Canada and Spain.

### Box 6.3. Principles and code of conduct for procurement in Spain and Canada

**Spain**

With the aim of contributing to excellence in administrative activities within the area of procurement, the Office for Supervision and Evaluation of Public Procurement has compiled in its code of conduct the basic principles and good practice that have already been integrated into the day-to-day activities of the ministries of the administration of the Generalitat of Catalonia and the entities that form part of its public sector. New content for establishing the code of conduct and recommendations is also contained, contributed by the Working Group for the Promotion and Improvement of Procurement Processes, constituted within the Consultative Board on Administrative Procurement of the Generalitat of Catalonia; the Anti-Fraud Office of Catalonia; the Catalan Competition Authority; the Association of Secretaries, Mediators and Treasurers of the Catalan Local Administration; as well as business and trade union organisations.

The aim of the code is to consolidate the code of ethics in procurement as part of the culture and values of procurement bodies. The good procurement practice included in the code is structured in the following sections:

1. the specifying of the basic principles and ethical values that must govern the procurement process
2. the identification of specific conduct of interest with a view to drawing up the guidelines to follow in a variety of possible real specific circumstances
3. the specifying of especially interesting contractual practices
4. the raising of awareness, training and the monitoring of the ethical commitment.

With the creation of the Ethics Committee in Procurement of the Generalitat of Catalonia, made up of representatives from the ministries and entities of the Generalitat of Catalonia and belonging to the Presidency Department, a follow up and continuous updating of the code in the administration of the Generalitat and the entities of its public sector will be carried out.

**Canada**

The Code of Conduct for Procurement provides all those involved in the procurement process – public servants and vendors alike – with a clear statement of mutual expectations to ensure a common basic understanding among all participants in accountable, ethical and transparent procurement. The Code of Conduct for Procurement applies to all transactions entered into by Public Works and Government Services of Canada (PWGSC) either for their own procurements or on behalf of a client department.

Box 6.3. **Principles and code of conduct for procurement in Spain and Canada** (*cont.*)

The Code of Conduct for Procurement gives guidance regarding:

- responsibilities of public servants
- conflict of interest measures
- post-employment measures
- vendors' responsibility regarding solicitation and contract provisions
- vendors' duty to respect the responsibilities of public servants
- vendor complaints and procedural safeguards
- sanctions.

*Sources:* Generalitat de Catalunya (2014), "Codi de principis i conductes recomanables en la contractació pública", (Principles and Code of Conduct for Procurement) http://presidencia.gencat.cat/web/ca/ambits_d_actuacio/oficina_de_supervisio_i_avaluacio_de_la_contractacio_publica_osacp/.content/osacp/baners/Aprovacio-Codi-conductes-recomanables.pdf (accessed 17 June 2015); Public Works and Government Services Canada (2014), "Context and purpose of the Code", www.tpsgc-pwgsc.gc.ca/app-acq/cndt-cndct/contexte-context-eng.html (accessed 6 May 2015).

In Costa Rica, there has recently been greater citizen engagement and participation through increased public consultations on projects. An example of this is the public consultation for the construction of an improved road intersection in La Uruca, connecting San José and Heredia. However, there is no institutionalised process for civil society to participate in the procurement process. Costa Rica could consider involving civil society formally through different stages of the procurement process, as done by Mexico (Box 6.4). Direct accountability to the public and other stakeholders is a fundamental means of increasing transparency and integrity in decision making. Maintaining a close dialogue with suppliers' organisations is essential to keep up-to-date information on market evolutions, reduce information asymmetry and improve value for money, in particular for high-value procurements. Keeping a direct and constant contact with the private sector may help the government to be aware of the burdens and barriers associated with the procurement process and find the best solutions to maximise taxpayers' money and reduce the possibilities to circumvent the law. Costa Rica could carry out an initiative similar to the one in the United States (Box 6.5).

Box 6.4. **Social witnesses in Mexico**

Since 2009, social witnesses are required to participate in all stages of public tendering procedures above certain thresholds as a way to promote public scrutiny. In 2014, these thresholds were MXN 336 million (approximately USD 25 million) for goods and services and MXN 672 million (approximately USD 50 million) for public works.

Social witnesses are non-government organisations and individuals selected by the Ministry of Public Administration through public tendering. The Ministry of Public Administration keeps a registry of the approved social witnesses and evaluates their performance; unsatisfactory performance potentially results in the removal of the social witness from the registry.

When a federal entity requires the involvement of a social witness, it informs the ministry, which designates one from the registry.

As of January 2014, the ministry had registered 39 social witnesses for public procurement

### Box 6.4. Social witnesses in Mexico *(cont.)*

projects: 5 civil society organisations and 34 individuals. This number has grown from 5 social witnesses in 2005 to almost 40 in 2014.

The Ministry of Public Administration notes that "the monitoring of the most relevant procurement processes of the federal government through social witnesses has had an impact in improving procurement procedures by virtue of their contributions and experience, to the point that they have become a strategic element for ensuring the transparency and credibility of the procurement system". An OECD-World Bank Institute study (2007) indicates that the participation of social witnesses in procurement processes of the Federal Electricity Commission (*Comisión Federal de Electricidad*) created savings of approximately USD 26 million in 2006 and increased the number of bidders by over 50%.

*Source:* OECD (2013), *Public Procurement Review of the Mexican Institute of Social Security: Enhancing Efficiency and Integrity for Better Health Care*, OECD Public Governance Reviews, OECD Publishing, Paris, http://dx.doi.org/10.1787/9789264197480-en.

### Box 6.5. "Welcome to the Open Dialogue" in the United States

The federal acquisition system is governed by a myriad of rules, both administrative and statutory, that are designed to help agencies maximise results from their contracts, make sure that contractors are qualified to do business with the federal government, and ensure consistency with key economic and social policies. Efforts to streamline, modernise and improve required procedures may allow contractors and agencies to execute in a more efficient and effective manner, while still supporting these policy objectives.

To identify potential improvements, the Chief Acquisition Officers Council (CAOC), in co-ordination with the Federal Acquisition Regulatory Council, the Chief Information Officers Council and the Office of Management and Budget's (OMB) Office of Federal Procurement Policy (OFPP), stood up an online platform in the second quarter of 2014 to allow members of the interested stakeholders acquisition community to engage with one another about burdens and barriers associated with the federal acquisition process and potential changes to address them.

This dialogue was part of an effort to improve the economy and efficiency of the federal acquisition system by identifying impactful steps that could be taken to make it easier for agencies to do business with the best companies and enter into contracts that allow these companies to provide their best solutions for the taxpayer.

The dialogue sought to identify specific rules and requirements, tools, procedures and practices that impact the efficiency and effectiveness of federal procurement and ways to improve them by encouraging responses in the following areas:

- Reporting and compliance requirements – e.g. opportunities where collection processes and systems can be re-engineered or automated, duplicative reporting can be eliminated, the frequency of reporting can be reduced and outdated compliance thresholds can be changed.
- Procurement practices – e.g. opportunities where acquisition strategies can be modernised (to support more efficient and effective acquisition of IT, in particular), where best commercial practices can be utilised, as well as efforts to promote greater consideration of innovative solutions and contracting practices.

**Box 6.5. "Welcome to the Open Dialogue" in the United States** *(cont.)*

- Participation by small and minority businesses, new entrants and non-traditional government contractors – e.g. opportunities for improving existing technical or strategic assistance programmes, making buying platforms for finding business opportunities and bidding more user friendly, and lowering the cost of doing business.

Using the online platform, interested parties submitted ideas, responded to questions posed by moderators and commented on other ideas – including those that they think are most promising and impactful.

*Source:* Chief Acquisition Officers Council (2014), "Open Dialogue on Improving How to Do Business with the Federal Government", http://cxo.dialogue.cao.gov.

## Recommendations

Costa Rica would benefit from agreeing on a single procurement platform that covers the whole public sector, including the autonomous entities. In order to ensure transparency, provide equal access to information for all suppliers, and promote competition and reinforce supplier trust, Costa Rica will need to ensure a proper integration of the different platforms. This would also require public official training and awareness raising.

The platform could also establish a system of red flags or mechanisms to track decisions and enable the identification of irregularities and potential corruption cases in public procurement.

The country could benefit from creating an authority to set a national procurement vision, work in a cohesive manner toward clear priorities and objectives. This public procurement authority could work closely with the different actors in order to consolidate goods and services and promote a more expansive use of framework agreements. An awareness campaign to establish trust and confidence among the different actors on the benefits of a procurement authority could be implemented.

Transparency of the procurement process could be enhanced through a series of practical measures, like the application of a unique set of thresholds for procurement procedures, clarification of good practices for contract clustering, and the development of a system to track decisions and enable the identification of irregularities and potential corruption cases.

Costa Rica could enhance the professionalisation of its procurement workforce. It could invest in providing adequate incentives to attract highly qualified officials and updating officials' knowledge and skills on a regular basis to reflect regulatory, management and technological evolutions. This could, for instance, be enhanced by developing a formal job description for procurement officials and introducing a specific code of conduct for them.

Costa Rica could enhance stakeholder involvement through the different stages of the procurement process.

## Notes

1. With the exception of non-state public entities financed by more than 50% by their own resources, contributions of its members, and public enterprises whose capital belongs mostly to private persons and not the public sector (Article 2, Procurement Act, Law 7494 of 1995).
2. Law to Strengthen the ICE.
3. See Law No. 8511 of 16 May 2006. The change was properly introduced in Article 15 of the Regulations of the Procurement Act, Executive Decree 3341-H of 2006.
4. See: www.hacienda.go.cr/docs/521ba66a1854b_Boletin%20de%20Convenio%20Marco%20Enero%202012-DGABCA.pdf.
5. Principle capacity: Ensure that procurement officials meet high professional standards for knowledge, practical implementation and integrity by providing a dedicated and regularly updated set of tools (OECD, 2015).

## *References*

Banco Nacional de Costa Rica (2010), "¿Qué es el mercado en línea Mer-link?", *ABC de Mer-Link*, www.bncr.fi.cr/BNCR/Proveeduria/PDF/BNCR%20-%20ABC%20MerLink.pdf.

Caddy et al. (2007), "Beyond Public Scrutiny: Stocktaking of Social Accountability in OECD Countries", OECD/World Bank Institute, http://www.oecd.org/gov/38983242.pdf (accessed 6 May 2015).

Chief Acquisition Officers Council (2014), "Open Dialogue on Improving How to Do Business with the Federal Government", http://cxo.dialogue.cao.gov.

Comptroller General of the Republic (2012), *Memoria Annual 2012* (*Annual Report 2012*), Comptroller General of the Republic, San José, www.cgr.go.cr/rev_dig/mem_anual/2012/files/assets/downloads/publicacion.pdf.

Gallup World Poll (n.d.), "Gallup World Poll", www.gallup.com/services/170945/world-poll.aspx.

Generalitat de Catalunya (2014), "Codi de principis i conductes recomanables en la contractació pública", (Principles and Code of Conduct for Procurement) http://presidencia.gencat.cat/web/ca/ambits_d_actuacio/oficina_de_supervisio_i_avalu

acio_de_la_contractacio_publica_osacp/.content/osacp/baners/Aprovacio-Codi-conductes-recomanables.pdf (accessed 17 June 2015).

INTOSAI (2010), "The Johannesburg Accords", XX INCOSAI South Africa, 27 November, INTOSAI, www.intosai.org/uploads/jhbaccordsen.pdf.

INTOSAI (1977), "The Lima Declaration of Guidelines on Auditing Precepts", International Standards of Supreme Audit Institutions 1, INTOSAI Professional Standards Committee, Copenhagen, www.issai.org/media/12901/issai_1_e.pdf.

OECD (2015), *OECD Recommendation of the Council on Public Procurement*, OECD, Paris, www.oecd.org/gov/ethics/recommendation-on-public-procurement.htm.

OECD (2014a), *Chile's Supreme Audit Institution: Enhancing Strategic Agility and Public Trust*, OECD Public Governance Reviews, OECD Publishing, Paris, http://dx.doi.org/10.1787/9789264207561-en.

OECD (2014b), *Spain: From Administrative Reform to Continuous Improvement*, OECD Public Governance Reviews, OECD Publishing, Paris, http://dx.doi.org/10.1787/9789264210592-en.

OECD (2013), *Public Procurement Review of the Mexican Institute of Social Security: Enhancing Efficiency and Integrity for Better Health Care*, OECD Public Governance Reviews, OECD Publishing, Paris, http://dx.doi.org/10.1787/9789264197480-en.

OECD (2009), *OECD Principles for Integrity in Public Procurement*, OECD Publishing, Paris, http://dx.doi.org/10.1787/9789264056527-en.

Public Works and Government Services Canada (2014), "Context and Purpose of the Code", www.tpsgc-pwgsc.gc.ca/app-acq/cndt-cndct/contexte-context-eng.html (accessed 6 May 2015).

Ruffner, M. and J. Sevilla (2004), "Public sector modernisation: Modernising accountability and control", *OECD Journal on Budgeting*, Vol. 4/2, pp. 123-141, OECD Publishing, Paris, http://dx.doi.org/10.1787/budget-v4-art11-en.

World Economic Forum (2014), "*The Global Competitiveness Report 2014-2015*", World Economic Forum, Geneva, www3.weforum.org/docs/WEF_GlobalCompetitivenessReport_2014-15.pdf.

# *Chapter 7*

# Improving multi-level governance in Costa Rica

*This chapter describes the importance of effective and efficient multi-level governance to enhance national development outcomes for citizens and businesses. It highlights that Costa Rica's multi-level governance is based on a mix of institutionally autonomous and territorially decentralised entities with currently very limited leverage for the latter, given the minimal level of public expenditure at the sub-national level and basic responsibilities in terms of public service production and delivery. It also studies the effectiveness of the Costa Rican constitutional reform of 2001 to allocate more functions and resources to local governments. The chapter suggests ways to improve the delivery of services across the territory, and close the urban-rural gap through the use of contracts to facilitate the functional relation between the central government and municipalities; the creation of a network of community agents providing local government with capacity building; and the introduction of flexibility in the governance system to help tailor policies to places.*

The statistical data for Israel are supplied by and under the responsibility of the relevant Israeli authorities. The use of such data by the OECD is without prejudice to the status of the Golan Heights, East Jerusalem and Israeli settlements in the West Bank under the terms of international law.

## Strong economic development since the 1990s, though unevenly distributed

Since the end of the 1990s, Costa Rica has experienced impressive economic development. Not only has the country been able to bounce back from a long-lasting crisis, but it has also been able to change its economic model, moving from an import substitution strategy to trade openness and foreign direct investment (FDI) attraction. As a result, citizens enjoy a good access to basic services, which is reflected in the fact that Costa Rica displays very good performance in indicators measuring national human development and well-being. Costa Rica is a regional champion in terms of citizen welfare and economic performance (OECD, 2006).

The industrial shift of the country – as a response to the economic crisis of the 1980s – is reflected in the export composition. FDI flows have played a crucial role in national development and continue to be important for the government. World-class multinational enterprises (MNEs) have invested in the country, among which Intel, which has transformed the country into a net exporter of integrated circuits and microprocessors (OECD, 2012). The process of attracting Intel to Costa Rica helped shape the country's investment promotion strategy and the way investment promotion was conducted. Fundamentally, new relationships were forged between the government, the Costa Rican Investment Promotion Agency (CINDE) and investors; a cohesion that helped Costa Rica land more investment and furthered improve the investment climate. Intel sent a strong signal to other investors that put Costa Rica on the global map, and served as an important ally in investment promotion (World Bank, 2006). After Intel's investment, several world-class businesses, including banks and insurance companies, localised key sections of their global value chains in Costa Rica.

Since the 1990s, Costa Rica has also become well-known as a destination for ecotourism. The country is a world leader in this sector and the number of visitors has doubled, reaching almost 2.4 million per year in the last decade. Tourism has allowed the country to employ the semi-skilled workforce, thus reducing unemployment in rural areas, which also have become less dependent on agriculture activities. Tourism also generates important flows of foreign exchange, which ease the pressure on the recurrent deficits in current accounts (OECD, 2006). For all these characteristics, tourism represents a perfect complement to the specialisation in knowledge-intense manufacturing, especially due to the fact that it concentrates in areas with low population density ("rural" according to the OECD definition) along the coasts.

Despite the overall economic progress, territorial imbalances have emerged and there is an important rural-urban split. There are several territorial communities – especially along the Caribbean and Pacific coast and other peripheral areas – that lag behind. Internal migration is putting pressure on the metropolitan region of San José, and this may choke economic growth.

Citizens and businesses have begun demanding a larger basket of public services, thus putting pressure on the current system, which is largely based on the institutionally decentralised sector producing standardised services for all citizens. Municipalities are searching to materialise the autonomy granted by law, and to reinforce their capacity, to be able to tailor services to local needs.

## Sub-national authorities with a minor role in the overall governance system

### *Municipalities as the only sub-national authorities with administrative powers*

When compared with OECD Members, Costa Rica's governance is based on a system in which the central level, and in particular the institutionally decentralised sector, plays a key role in delivering policies and services, while sub-national authorities – including municipalities – are marginal. Costa Rica is a unitary country composed of seven provinces. Provinces are divided into 81 administrative units (*cantones*), each of them directed by a mayor who is elected every 4 years. The lower administrative level includes 423 districts. Only the central government and municipalities (or *cantones*) have administrative powers. The seven provinces are basically mere electoral districts and are used to organise voters and their political representatives. Finally, the planning system of Costa Rica, created in the 1970s, introduced six planning regions which implement territory-specific components of the national development strategy set at the central level. Planning regions host regional development councils, formed by representatives of the central government, which approve, execute and monitor regional development plans (the Limón Province Council is currently the most active one).

The Constitution allocates a large, yet undefined, power to municipalities. Their action is mostly framed and organised by the central government and national regulation. The general principles of territorial decentralisation are set forth in the Political Constitution. Since 1949 several reforms have strengthened sub-national governments. Since 1998, local governments have been elected directly by citizens and are perceived as key stakeholders by the public. In general, municipalities are responsible for managing and providing some municipal public services; setting and collecting municipal fees and taxes; convening citizens to popular consultations; promoting participatory and inclusive local development; and advancing local public policies in favour of gender equality. Some municipal governments are responsible for administrating a large territory, which encompasses a large number of districts. By agreement with other municipalities or with the appropriate government agency or body, the municipality may carry out, jointly or individually, services or works in the canton or region. Finally, the municipality has the authority to dictate the urban regulatory plan and all guidelines pertaining to spatial planning. However, the constitutional mandate is very broad and general, meaning that municipalities are not in charge of a specific policy or public sector.

Local governments raise their own taxes. For most municipalities, their own taxes represent the greatest source of revenues. Municipalities are entitled to collect municipal taxes such as property tax (real estate), register (patents) and services provided to citizens (waste collection, for instance). Besides their own taxes, municipalities also receive transfers from the central level. In fact, the Constitution states that the central level has to transfer funds to local governments. According to the legal framework (Laws No. 7755 and 8114), the government allocates transfers to municipalities based on criteria such as the extension, population and position of the social development index of the municipalities, though this is not necessarily the perception of stakeholders, as expressed during interviews.

Compared with the OECD average, Costa Rica's public expenditure is low; the institutionally decentralised sector accounts for a large share of it, while the territorially decentralised sector only accounts for a minor share. In particular, sub-national expenditure is low in all domains, meaning that Costa Rica's territorial authorities play a marginal role in delivering policies and services to their communities, including direct investment or public procurement; representing a fraction of the average contribution of sub-national authorities in OECD Members.

Figure 7.1. **Public expenditure by the territorially decentralised sector in Costa Rica**

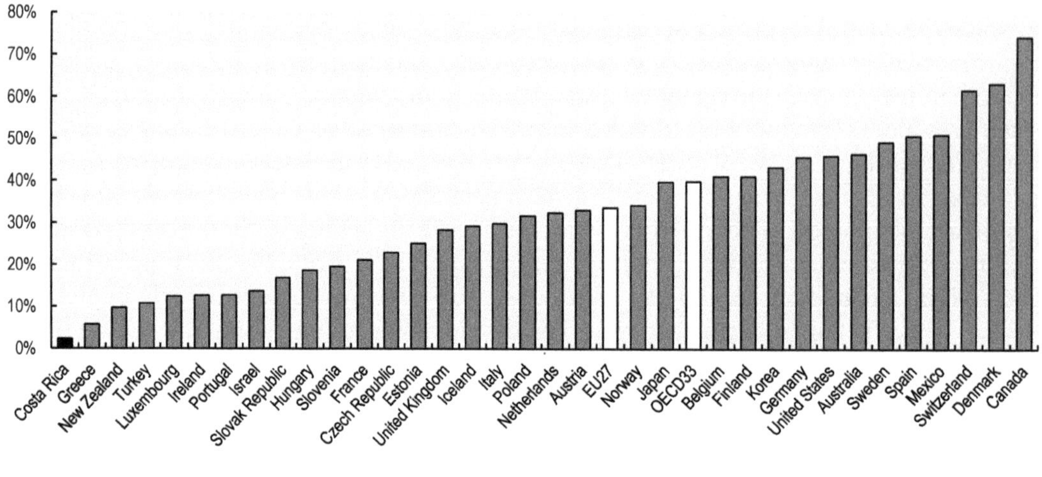


*Source:* Government of Costa Rica (2014), "Background report", unpublished working paper and OECD data.

## *The role of federations of municipalities and cantonal councils for co-ordination*

Most of Costa Rica's municipalities are organised in federations. These intermediate institutions – which were introduced in Costa Rica by the Municipal Code of 1970 – can have different aims. For instance, some of them have the purpose to lobby in favour of local governments with the central power, in order to promote decentralisation of power in the country. Other federations work to scale up policies and services to larger territorial communities. Finally, there are federations that provide a common framework to national and local institutions operating within a common territory. Currently, there are 12 federations in Costa Rica. All of them possess legal personality, and have their own budget and administrative autonomy.

Federations may represent an asset for Costa Rica's multi-level governance system. In particular, there are some federations that play an important role in Costa Rica's governance. One of them is FEDOMA (*Federación Occidental de Municipalidades de Alajuela*). FEDOMA federates 11 municipalities in the central region, including Alajuela, which is the second-largest city in Costa Rica. The federation is active in promoting decentralisation in the country and provides its members with capacity-building activities in several fields. Another important federation is the FGLCFN, which is active in the north of the country, in the area bordering Nicaragua. This is a poor area of the country, which is based on agriculture and did not benefit from the development of the country related to FDIs or tourism activities. The local population suffers from the lack of good infrastructure and services, and the three municipalities in the area are experiencing a net demographic loss. Taking advantage of the recent national policy *Tejiendo Desarrollo* (Box 7.1) – which could be translated as "weaving development" and whose aim is to support locally created development initiatives – the federation has started functioning as a regional development agency, which promotes very specific development interventions in the area.

### Box 7.1. Tejiendo Desarrollo: "Weaving development"

*Tejiendo Desarrollo* is a policy framework supporting community-led development processes, which was recently introduced in Costa Rica. The objectives of the network are the following: to promote the participation of civil society in development processes, to articulate the sectoral organisation of the government and to design policies that respond to the priorities of local actors.

The National Development Plan describes the network and its two key components: to promote development processes in specific territories (10 territories which comprise 34 cantons) and to develop a National Policy on Regional and Territorial Development with civil society participation led by the Ministry of National Planning and Economic Policy (Ministerio de Planificación Nacional y Política Económica, MIDEPLAN).

The following institutions are part of the core group of this network: Office of the First Lady, MIDEPLAN, the Institute of Municipal Development and Assistance, the Rural Development Institute and the National Directorate for Community Development

The extended network counts the participation of the Ministry of Agriculture and Livestock ), Ministry of Public Works and Transport , the Joint Social Welfare Institute , the Ministry of Work, the Ministry of Housing and Urban Development , the Ministry of Culture, the – Vice-Ministry of Youth, the National Institute for Women, the National Commission for Emergencies, National Institute of Rural and Urban Housing , National Institute for Vocational Training , Costa Rican Tourism Board, Vice-Ministry of Telecommunications, Ministry of Environment and Energy , Costa Rican Institute for Water Supply and Sewerage , National System of Conservation Areas , Ministry of Economy, Industry and Trade, Ministry of Sports.

*Source:* Decree No. 38536 of 2015 and Directive No. 006 of 2015.

However, Costa Rica's system of municipal federation faces a series of challenges that should be dealt with to take full advantage of these intermediate institutions. According to the International City/County Management Association (2004), the system of federations suffers from the fact that most federations do not have strategic plans (vision or mission) that integrate the shared interest of their members. This causes their inactivity. Another key problem is that several federations were created under the influence of national organisations, non-governmental organisations and international co-operation agencies. So, they are not the product of a bottom-up process. Third, not all of the members of a given federation are treated in the same way and the strongest municipalities have used federations to gain political influence in a larger territory.

The cantonal councils for inter-institutional co-ordination (*Consejo Cantonal de Coordinación Institucional*, CCCI) are another type of intermediate institutions, created to co-ordinate sectorial policies at the municipal level. As of 2015, 51 municipalities – out of the total of 81 – have created their CCCI. CCCIs involve representatives from the central government and other public institutions in charge of delivering services at the municipal level, including autonomous agencies. All CCCIs have a technical secretariat that produces a co-ordination plan based on the needs of the municipalities and on the feedback of the institutional bodies involved in the council. Mayors have the role of facilitating the implementation of these plans, thus taking over the role of co-ordinators of other institutions active in the territory they govern. The central government – i.e. MIDEPLAN – provides councils with technical support, monitoring and evaluation activities, but not with funds; municipalities have to cover the operating costs of CCCIs.

CCCIs have the potential to become key hubs within the national governance system, but they are still confronted with important challenges. CCCIs are the product of a bottom-up process, triggered by local mayors. Also, cantonal councils respond to a key need of Costa Rica's governance: improve the co-ordination of autonomous agencies and between them and local government. Finally, CCCIs contribute to the knowledge pooling – which means that all stakeholders accept to put together information to lead policy making (Barca, 2001) – the country needs to orient public investment choices at a time at which the government is trying to design and implement a new economic strategy that follows up to the one based on FDI attraction. However, challenges remain. First, poor municipalities may lack capacities and funds to create CCCIs. This is particularly true for poor rural municipalities which often do not have the resources to guarantee the functioning of the institution (an office, some basic human resources, etc.). In these cases there is a need for support, at least for the first years of functioning of CCCIs. Second, representatives from public companies and autonomous agencies do not always recognise the technical leadership of local mayors and the CCCI secretariat, which negatively affects the capacity of councils to co-ordinate policies. Third, citizens have limited possibilities to participate in the councils. The possibility to involve local stakeholders, including private business, has been initially ignored by the legislator, who considered the presence of the mayor as sufficient to represent all the instances of local constituencies in a given CCCI. Only recently has the law been amended to give citizens the possibility to play a more active role in these local instances.

## The important role of the institutionally decentralised sector

Compared with the OECD average, Costa Rica's public expenditure is low; the institutionally decentralised sector accounts for a large share of it, while the territorially decentralised sector is a minor one. In particular, sub-national expenditure is low in all domains, meaning that Costa Rica's territorial authorities play a marginal role in delivering policies and services to their communities, including direct investment or public procurement; representing a fraction of the average contribution of sub-national authorities in OECD Members.

A large part of public expenditure is executed by the institutionally decentralised sector that is in charge of producing key services. The institutionally decentralised sector is a key actor of Costa Rica's multi-level governance system and delivers services mostly related to Costa Rica's social welfare system, such as healthcare, food security, child care, etc. Within this system, institutionally decentralised institutions execute about 50% of total public expenditure. The institutionally decentralised sector has substantially contributed to the good performance of Costa Rica in terms of access to basic services, but the large number of institutions may cause duplication, put pressure on public expenditure and also limit co-ordination among sectorial policies and between levels of government. Major institutions include, for instance, IMAS – which tops the ranking and is in charge of cash transfers and pro-poor policies. In 2012, IMAS generated more than 1% of Costa Rican public expenditure. Another important agency is PANI (Patronato Nacional de la Infancia), which is in charge of child welfare throughout the country. PANI serves all children and adolescents residing in Costa Rica. PANI is organised in a network of territorial offices, located in all provinces. Another important agency is the National Council for Rehabilitation and Special Education (Consejo Nacional de Rehabilitación y Educación Especial, CNREE), whose purpose is to plan, co-ordinate, advise and oversee the activities of all social actors involved in the inclusive development of people with disabilities.

## Emerging challenges

Costa Rica has been successful over the past two decades, but new challenges are emerging that are questioning the institutional framework to achieve economic performance. For instance, the human geography of Costa Rica has become more complex, regional disparities and an evident urban-rural split are emerging. Due to economic development, citizens demand a larger basket of public services, which is also diversified according to their specific needs. Costa Rica has also to deal with exogenous forces. For instance, international competition to attract FDIs in knowledge-intensive industries has been dramatically increasing, also from other Latin American countries. Key partners such as Intel and Bank of America have decided to reduce their investment in Costa Rica and this may influence the behaviour of other international players. Export competition in traditional sectors related to tropical agriculture is also mounting.

### *Lower access to basic public services for rural poor population*

The rural poor population has, on average, less access to basic public services. Accessibility to public services depends on income and location. Reduced access to basic services has territorial features: according to Trejos (2008), there is a difference between accessibility to education in urban and rural areas. The share of households with no access to basic services (including water sanitation, healthcare and primary education) is almost four times lower in the Central planning region (which is where the capital San José is located) than in the regions of Huetar Caribe and Huetar Norte, which are the poorest and most rural territories in the country. The urban-rural split in terms of service accessibility is also reflected in Costa Rica's Social Development Index (composed of eleven socioeconomic indicators), with stronger performance situated in urban areas.

Figure 7.2. **Social Development Index in Costa Rica**

By municipality and district, 2013 | By socioeconomic region and district, 2013

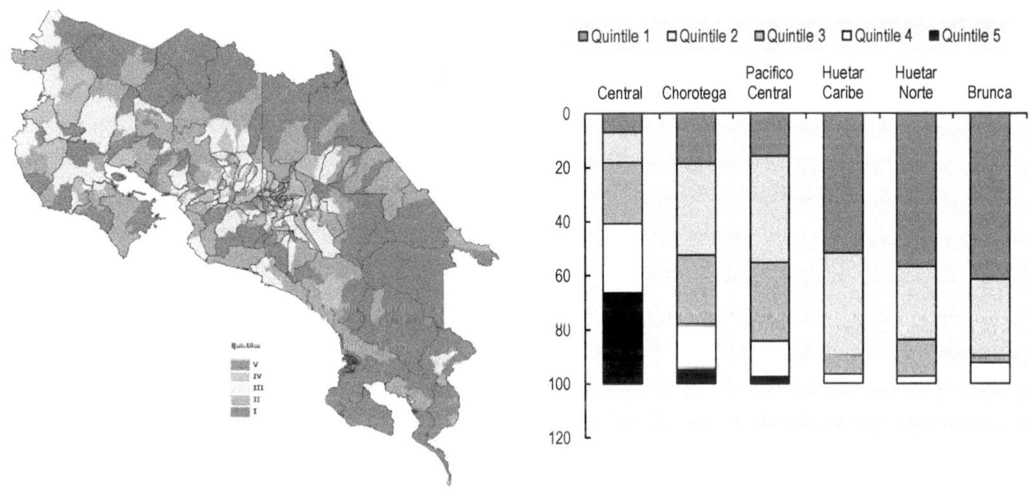


*Note:* This map is without prejudice to the status of or sovereignty over any territory, to the delimitation of international frontiers and boundaries and to the name of any territory, city or area.

*Source:* MIDEPLAN (2013), "Indice de desarrollo social", http://www.mideplan.go.cr/component/content/category/249:indice-de-desarrollo-social-2013.html.

It is not clear whether the state meets the actual expectations of citizens in terms of accessibility to services and public goods. There could be at least three shortcomings in the current system *vis-à-vis* citizens. First, it may fail to provide citizens in different areas of the country with tailored services (i.e. the current rural-urban split). Second, it may negatively affect co-ordination of sectorial policies. For instance, as different services such as education and transport are dealt with by different agencies, co-ordination of policy delivery – especially when done in non-urban areas – is limited by the lack of a common institutional framework. Third, it is not clear to whom autonomous agencies are accountable. Lack of accountability in the public sector may cause low participation rates in Costa Rica. According to the UNDP (2013), the country has the lowest participation rates in the region.

Costa Ricans have developed negative expectations about the future performance of the public sector. According to a recent research done by the UNDP (2013), a significant percentage of Costa Ricans considers that the quality of basic services, including education and in particular healthcare – two sectors in which the country has a positive record of improvement – will decline in the next decade. The negative perception could also depend on the fact that the process of devolution of powers to municipalities is largely incomplete. Since 1998, citizens can elect their mayors. As shown above, this gave them the impression that municipalities – which can be considered as the forefront of the government as a whole – can have an impact on public policies. This is a false perception that puts pressure on the local governments and also gives citizens the impression of a dysfunctional public sector. There are also negative expectations concerning the possibility to participate in the public sector, which confirm the scarce level of accountability in the current governance system.

### *Foreign direct investment and tourism have developed weak linkages with local businesses*

FDIs and tourism have developed weak linkages with local businesses and current trends in Costa Rica's productive framework challenge the national governance system. In 2014, key investors, including Intel, decided to drastically reduce their activities in Costa Rica. A number of assessments of Costa Rica's economy (OECD, 2013; Paus and Gallagher, 2006; Cordero and Paus, 2008) illustrate the limited extent of backward linkages from FDI and identify two main causes: limited potential for spillovers for part of the foreign investment and the limited domestic absorptive capacity for linkages. Surveys administered to suppliers and multinational enterprises in Costa Rica revealed few cases of positive technology transfer from an MNE to its suppliers (Alfaro and Rodríguez-Clare, 2004). It is possible that, despite being successful in attracting FDIs, the country has lacked a coherent long-term development strategy. Cordero and Paus (2008) identify a structural problem in Costa Rica's strategy to attract FDI: it has been based on tax cuts and trade liberalisation. These measures may not be compatible with a long-term development strategy that develops the country's ability to create and maintain an adequate stock of country-specific assets of the type that are required for the continuous attraction of FDI flows.

The country may also fail to take advantage of its full potential in tourism activities. The success of tourism depends on large-scale developments – hotels/resorts with a large number of accommodation realised by international investors – rather than on local small and medium-sized businesses (Peralta Quesada and Solano Umanzor, 2009). This model puts pressure on natural amenities and – as in the case of FDIs – may fail to involve national actors in a process of long-term sustainable development. Local stakeholders –

mayors of tourist municipalities – met during a study visit mentioned that the autonomous agency in charge of road maintenance in their territories do not consult with them and concentrate their interventions on roads that are not important for tourists visiting the area. Although anecdotal, this feedback questions the capacity of the national autonomous agencies to deal with the changing social and economic environment of the country.

In practice, what happens in Costa Rica is that, with the exception of the metal-mechanic and plastics sectors, foreign tech companies make most of their purchases of local products and services in non-critical areas such as labels and packaging or support activities like security, cleaning and food. Foreign companies have demonstrated little interest to develop a network of local suppliers, for reasons of economies of scale, trust and quality control (OECD, 2013). Costa Rica may need to put in place a policy to improve backward linkages between MNEs and local businesses. This requires an all-round industrial strategy which is also based on the capacity to deliver policies and services – including infrastructure and higher education – to regions where the MNEs and potential suppliers are located.

Sub-national governments are not prepared to deliver tailored public services and promote regional development. This is due to lack of capacities and also financial resources. It is possible that the presence of the agencies, which in some cases have territorial offices, may have caused a sort of institutional inertia in local governments that have limited their activities to a very limited number of sectors. In fact, the only sectors in which municipalities have exclusive responsibility are "treatment of waste" and "public adornment" (Government of Costa Rica, 2014). Public authorities may need to pool information together with sub-national stakeholders, including municipalities and districts, in order to be able to design and deliver effective policies to all citizens, regardless their location in the country.

## Promoting inclusive growth and reducing regional disparities through multi-level governance

The national reforms of the multi-level governance system go in the right direction but need to be implemented, and to involve sub-national authorities. Costa Rica is committed to improve service accessibility and policy delivery across the country. Public authorities are knowledgeable about the need to keep improving the performance of the public sector to promote inclusive growth in the country. Within this context, a long series of institutional reforms have been implemented with the aim to promote the role of municipalities (and intermediate levels) within the national governance system. In 1970, a reform transformed municipal executives into mayors elected by municipal councils. The regulation evolved again in 1998, when the new municipal code allowed citizens to vote for the mayor. According to national stakeholders, the reform did not have the expected impact over citizen engagement with public policies. In the three elections held after the reform – 2002, 2006 and 2010 – participation rates were 23%, 24% and 27.9%, respectively. Although there are regional differences, the average level remains very low. It is possible that the situation will improve in 2016, when a new system of local election – with a time lag of two years with respect to national elections – will be put in place. In 2001, there was a key constitutional reform which allocated more functions and resources to municipalities. In particular, the reform established a progressive and automatic increase of the share of public revenues allocated to municipalities. This should have achieved 10% of the government budget – excluding the budget allocated to autonomous agencies – once completed. The reform did not modify the fiscal basis at the municipal level, meaning that the additional resources should have been transferred from the central government.

The reform process has stalled since 2001, and most reforms have remained basically "on paper". The result is that municipalities continue having a marginal role within Costa Rica's public sector, and this despite their increased visibility *vis-à-vis* citizens, as assessed above. Moreover, the lack of implementation hasgenerated uncertainty in the system. This is the case of the constitutional reform of 2001, which allocated more responsibility to municipalities but did not modify their capacity to collect fiscal revenues in their communities. More importantly, the new competences of municipalities overlap with those of some autonomous agencies, so there is need for co-ordination. However, the attempts to improve policy co-ordination, in particular through the CCCIs, have been relatively unsuccessful.

In 2014, a new government put decentralisation and governance among the priorities of its activity and started working to implement past reforms. The new political orientation depends on the large regional disparities, and in particular on the urban-rural split, which are becoming more and more evident in the country. This approach is reflected in the National Development Plan for 2015-18. The NDP has identified three strategic priorities: promote national growth and jobs; reduce poverty rates; improve the public sector's openness, transparency and accountability. The programming document illustrates key differences in terms of service accessibility at the regional level and in particular the existing split between the metropolitan area of San José (Región Central) and the rest of the country.[1] It also discusses the quality of services, rather than merely looking at the quantity (or production). The fact that the policy looks at these dimensions – accessibility and quality – triggers the need of adopting a more place-based approach to policy making which requires better vertical and horizontal co-ordination within the public sector. The NDP also mentions the importance of involving local stakeholders and constituencies in the definition and delivery of policies. This is another aspect that requires the actual devolution of responsibilities, resources and capacities to sub-national communities.

The recently established network controlled by the Presidency of the Republic of Costa Rica – *Tejiendo Desarrollo* (see Box 7.1) – brought about important innovations in the national approach to multi-level governance. A first key innovation is the focus on rural and peripheral areas. Over the past decades, public policies have supported urbanisation and in particular the area of San José. The new policy approach aims at closing the gap between rural and urban in terms of service delivery and economic opportunities, also taking into account the increasing importance of economic activities such as tourism and industrial agriculture (pineapple for instance). This connects with a second important innovation, which relates to the role of FDI within the national economy. While attracting foreign investors topped the agenda of Costa Rica's governments since 1990s, the current government is more focused on the valorisation of national assets and investment opportunities. Policy supporting national economic actors may, in fact, help in developing backward linkages between FDIs and local suppliers. A third innovation in the system is the focus on capacity building for sub-national authorities and in particular for municipalities. National authorities consider capacity building as a key challenge for multi-level governance. However, although promising, a key limit of the current approach may be represented by the limited direct involvement of municipalities or their federations. In this sense, the governance adjustments that are currently explored are closer to the concept of deconcentration of national authorities rather than devolution of government powers.

## Recommendations

The government has to identify an efficient level of decentralisation for the country. In general, a first step to assess the performance of decentralisation (or centralisation) arrangements is to identify clearly who is in charge of what, in terms of design, regulation, budget and implementation in the policy sector that government wishes to improve. Triviality in this "institutional mapping" approach is merely apparent: many actors will be seen at first glance to be overlapping in their functions with others, while being dependent on others' decisions and being influenced by the use of one administrative tool or another. Overlapping per se is not a concern if co-ordination among stakeholders in public policy delivery is effective. If not, various co-ordination "gaps" can explain some failure in efficiently managing public policies. The national government may need to carefully assess the current governance system in order to identify these institutional "holes".

### *Use contracts to facilitate the functional relation between the central government and municipalities*

The implementation of the governance reform in Costa Rica seems to be challenged by a vicious cycle: the central government, including agencies, cannot allocate more responsibilities to municipalities as they lack capacities; however, municipalities cannot acquire new capacity without experiencing more responsibilities. To break this dynamic, the national authority may consider the use of contracts. The advantage of a contract is that it helps identify a specific task to devolve to a given municipality. It clarifies the scope of the devolved activity and even its timeline, if relevant. Finally, the contract also helps clarify the expected outcome, thus facilitating monitoring and evaluation and contributing to the enhancement of institutional trust (routine).

Contracts could be extended to other institutional entities, besides municipalities. For instance, federations of municipalities could be part of a contract with the national government, and be in charge of supporting municipalities in the delivery of a given service. Federations could provide tailored capacity-building activities or other tasks related to information co-ordination, monitoring, communication, etc. Involving them would provide them with a scope and a clear mission. CCCIs are other entities that could be part of a contract between municipalities and the national government and take over specific tasks related to the delivery of a given service or policy.

There are several examples of inter-institutional contracts that Costa Rican authorities could take into account. For instance, a good practice is that of Colombia's *contratos plan* (Box 7.2). These contracts are binding agreements signed by the central government and sub-national authorities that commit together to deliver policy interventions that are coherent with the regional development strategy (and then with the National Development Plan of Colombia). In particular, these contracts provide sub-national authorities, including departments (Colombia's intermediate tier of government) and municipalities with targeted financial resources and with capacity building: the possibility to learn how to improve policy delivery through a learning-by-doing process. It is worth noting that in the example, the central government considers municipalities as peers and does not take advantage of its larger capacity and position in the legal framework to impose strict conditions on sub-national governments.

### *Create a network of community agents providing local government with capacity building*

As discussed above, Costa Rica has become a dual country in which there is a relatively rich metropolitan region and rural territories that tend to lag behind. This split depends also on the lack of capacity in rural regions, which affects the capacity of these territories to capitalise on their assets. As the government is trying to reorient the economic strategy of the country and tone down the focus on FDI attraction, it would need to promote the development of untapped resources, including natural amenities and manufacturing in peripheral areas. The current governance system limits this possibility as it does not provide the centre with the needed information about local potential, which is necessary to orient investment decisions.

#### Box 7.2. *Contratos plan* in Colombia

Colombia's *contratos plan* is a governance tool that helps align investment agendas at the national and local level, improving accountability and transparency and providing sub-national authorities with capacity building. The contract is a binding agreement between the central government and a department, a group of departments or a group of municipalities. The parties commit to co-ordinate their investment agendas among sectors and across tiers of governments. In addition, they agree to deliver their interventions within a given timeline.

Colombia's negotiated territorial development is part of a broader national strategy whose aim is to create institutions and capacity that can support development policies. Contracts were introduced in 2012 by the national Law on Land Use (*Ley Orgánica de Ordenamiento Territorial*, LOOT) and by the National Development Plan 2010-2014, "*Prosperidad para Todos*". The LOOT is a key achievement for Colombia because it demonstrates that public authorities have regained control of the national territory after decades of conflict. Its intent is to improve Colombia's multi-level governance, and provides public authorities with flexible governance instruments to deliver policy interventions where they are needed the most. The *contrato plan* was instituted as a result of the 2011 reform of royalty payments. This important reform distributes revenues generated by extractive activities to all departments in the country. Sub-national authorities can use this additional revenue to co-finance interventions listed in the contracts. Finally, contracts also connect with innovative approaches to rural development that seek to improve service delivery to poor households in remote communities.

As of 2013, seven *contrato plans* had been signed in Colombia, for a total (anticipated) investment of USD 6.7 billion, over five years. The policy affects almost 6 million citizens, most of whom live in rural/remote areas in nine departments. The contracts identify infrastructure, and in particular road connectivity, as their main objective. Basic services such as healthcare, education and water sanitation are also priorities. While these objectives are supported by national transfers earmarked by the central government to all departments and municipalities, the contracts add flexibility to the policy and allow sub-national authorities to tailor action to their specific needs. In short, departments and municipalities have more funds, the possibility of co-ordinating different sources of investment from different levels of government (co-financing mechanisms) and improved capacity to promote development and fight poverty.

Contracts are not a panacea in the Colombian context, but they have generated some positive results. For instance, they have "reactivated" development planning at the department level. Department plans, in fact, identify measures to be taken within the contracts. Another key advantage is the opportunity for learning that the contracts provide departmental governments. They offer sub-national authorities the possibility of working with national representatives as they execute the measures, including large infrastructure projects. In general, contracts are a first attempt in Colombia to connect spatial planning with development policy.

*Source*: OECD (2014), *OECD Territorial Reviews: Colombia 2014*, OECD Publishing, Paris, http://dx.doi.org/10.1787/9789264224551-en.

The lack of a knowledge-pooling system is a challenge faced by several OECD Members. In the Canadian province of Quebec, for instance, many rural communities were suffering from structural economic and demographic decline due to job losses in sectors they were depending on such as forestry or fishery. The provincial government was trying to provide them with help, but was unable to identify alternative economic specialisations. So, it decided to create an extended and co-ordinated network of development agents to provide declining rural communities with the capacity to self-identify development opportunities and set policies accordingly. Once territorial development strategies were set, the provincial government was able to successfully allocate financial help to rural communities (Box 7.3).

**Box 7.3. Quebec's experience with development agents supporting rural territories**

In Quebec, the provincial government has implemented a rural development policy – the Rural Pact – that aims to strengthen technical capacity (programming), social capital and participation in sparsely populated regions. This requires that each community identify a seven-year development plan and use funds from the centre to carry it out. Rural development agents are essential in this framework for creating a vision for local development in territorial communities and helping policy implementation and monitoring, to guarantee accountability. Rural development agents help local committees and project promoters in developing investment projects, facilitate knowledge sharing and help monitor the national rural development policy. County governments or regional development centres can hire the agents financed by the government of Quebec's rural pact commitments.

The 136 current agents receive annual updated training, organised by the advisory body Solidarité Rurale du Québec and financed by Quebec's Ministry of Rural Development and Land Occupation. This training includes annual meetings of agents from all over the province and an interactive online portal that facilitates the exchange of experiences. The commitment, qualification and experience of rural development agents, along with a competitive salary, are important for their success. It is the agents' responsibility to link local project developers with county governments and municipalities, but also to develop connections between project developers and the funding instruments available in the regional development centres. Since successful local development depends on a community's capacity to facilitate connections across different socio-economic groups, the agents also have a major role to play in building bridges between social and economic development and creating teams of people and groups in a given territory who otherwise do not necessarily interact. Finally, the collective experience of the network of rural agents is important for the government's efforts to develop its rural development policy; it was consulted, for instance, in preparing the second round of the seven-year rural policy, in 2007. The funding provided by the Directorate for Public Governance and Territorial Development is a critical element. To guarantee that qualified people are hired, and to avoid excessive turnover, development agents are well compensated. Funds are provided by both the provincial government and county governments. In counties where development challenges are more intense, the provincial government assumes the largest share of the salaries, and can also provide the community with several agents.

*Source:* OECD (2010b), *Rural Development Policy Reviews: Québec, Canada 2010*, OECD Publishing, Paris, http://dx.doi.org/10.1787/9789264224551-en.

This good practice could inspire Costa Rica's governance and regional development policy. Providing lagging territories with community developers could help promote trust in government while also improving citizen participation, which is considered to be low in the country. For instance, Costa Rica could promote the generalisation of CCCIs to all territories, including rural areas. The central level could allocate some funds to those municipalities that do not have the possibility to cover the operating costs of the council.[2] In order to promote standardisation and exchange of information, CCCIs could be networked by MIDEPLAN, which would serve as central hub and would be in charge of training the agents to be sent to municipalities. Agents would provide local mayors with technical information and support to deal with public companies and autonomous agencies. Federations of municipalities may also be involved to connect local experiences and identify good policy practices across municipalities. CCCIs should involve citizens and non-governmental organisations in the identification of key local assets and economic drivers, which should be taken into account in local development strategies. This may positively affect social capital in the country and help increase trust in the government, since municipalities are the forefront of the public sector.

### *Introducing flexibility in the governance system could help tailor policies to places*

Despite its relatively small size, Costa Rica is a diverse country in which territorial communities face different challenges and opportunities. Within this context, a policy that would be effective in promoting the development of the metropolitan area of San José may have no impact in a rural territory on the Atlantic coast. This depends on the different economic framework, but also on the different sets of skills that are possessed by local governments and institutions. Regional diversity is evident when assessing the quality of specific public services such as education, which tend to be lower in rural areas, as discussed above. For all of these reasons, Costa Rica needs to put in place a governance system that is able to generate a range of policies that adapt to the different features of the communities they intend to serve. This requires flexibility and also the possibility to experiment with different territorial systems.

Policy diversity (in response to regional diversity) is a common feature in OECD Members. There are Members like Germany or Italy that have been dealing for several decades with structural dualism in their country, and that were forced to create a very different policy and governance framework to respond to the different needs of territories: on the one hand, competitive regions able to compete at the global scale; and on the other hand regions suffering from the lack of basic infrastructure and services.

Despite being a small and relatively homogenous country, Costa Rica may benefit from Sweden's experience with "variable-geometry" governance. This flexible system has allowed adjusting the policy reform to the characteristics of the different regions (densely populated cities vs. sparsely populated rural areas; Box 7.4). The result is that the country has been able to promote the competitiveness of urban areas, while also providing rural remote areas with investment and tailored social policies. As in the case of Sweden, Costa Rica needs to promote economic development in rural areas, without compromising the competitiveness of its main urban hub. There is evidence (OECD, 2015) that institutional fragmentation reduces the economic performance of metropolitan areas, causing lower productivity levels. Conversely, rural areas – characterised by low population densities – benefit from local institutions as these facilitate policy co-ordination and provide them with voice and visibility *vis-à-vis* the central government. Accordingly, rural Costa Rica may benefit from intermediate institutions active in peripheral areas. The current regional development network, led by the Presidency of the Republic, may promote territorial experiments in which different governance mechanisms are implemented.

### Box 7.4. Sweden implements bottom-up governance reform to experiment with different solutions

The case of Sweden illustrates that a country can experiment with multi-level governance with a trial and error process. In Sweden, government power is allocated mostly to municipalities and the central level. However, pressures to change the system have increased since the mid-1990s, particularly with the entry of Sweden into the European Union in 1995 and the new direction of Swedish regional policy. Sweden's decentralisation has been a largely bottom-up process, as the national government has not imposed a single model on the counties. A bottom-up strategy is uncommon in OECD Members, as most local government reforms have been imposed by the national government.

Since the late 1990s, Sweden has developed different regionalisation options in different regions, i.e. decentralisation has been pursued in an asymmetric manner. There have been three "waves" of regionalisation reforms:

- The first took place from 1997/98 to 2002, with the creation of "pilot regions" in Västra Götaland (three counties including the city of Göteborg) and Skåne (with Malmö as its main centre). In these regions, directly elected regional councils have taken over responsibility for regional development from the county administrative boards. Directly elected regional bodies also have responsibility for former tasks of the county councils (mainly healthcare). This phase has been described as a trial of limited duration and scope. However, because of strong regional support, the regional pilot project was prolonged for Skåne and Västra Götaland after 2002.
- The second wave (2002-07) was less ambitious in scope. The national government no longer pushed for the creation of pilot regions with a full set of competencies for regional development but to form regional co-ordination bodies (depending on the agreement of municipalities). The regional co-ordination bodies are indirectly elected and funded by a member fee. They are also partially funded by the national government for the tasks taken over from the county administrative boards. They are responsible for co-ordinating regional development work and deciding upon certain government envelopes for regional development and infrastructure planning, such as roads and the broadband network. The members of the regional co-ordination bodies can also decide that the council should focus on other issues, such as public transport, cultural institutions, tourism, business development and international co-operation.
- The third wave, took place between 2007 and 2009. It can be described as a renewed bottom-up demand for regionalisation. This reform gives adjacent counties the possibility to merge and convert themselves into regional authorities. The government supported the extension of the pilot region model to all Swedish regions, to simplify and harmonise territorial governance.

*Source*: OECD (2010a), *Territorial Policy Reviews: Sweden 2010*, OECD Publishing, Paris, http://dx.doi.org/10.1787/9789264081888-en.

## Notes

1. For instance, citizens living in the Región Central have up to two years of schooling more than citizens living in other areas of the country. Likewise, healthcare coverage is very good in the metropolitan area of the capital, but challenging in rural areas, where some 20% of citizens are not covered by the national health system.

2. This would be a way to allocate the increasing funds the central government is supposed to transfer to municipalities, as indicated by the 2001 reform of the Constitution.

## *References*

Alfaro, L. and A. Rodriguez-Clare (2004), "Multinationals and linkages: An empirical investigation", *Journal of LACEA Economia,* Vol. 4, No. 2, Spring, pp. 143-169, Brookings Institution Press, www.jstor.org/stable/20065460.

Barca, F. (2001), "New trends and policy shift in the Italian Mezzogiorno", in: Daedalus, *Italy Resilient and Vulnerable, Volume 1: The European Challenge*.

Cordero, J. and E. Paus (2008), "Foreign investment and economic development in Costa Rica: The unrealized potential", Working Group on Development and Environment in the America, Discussion Paper Number 13, https://ase.tufts.edu/gdae/Pubs/rp/DP13Paus_CorderoApr08.pdf.

Government of Costa Rica (2014), "Background report", unpublished working paper.

International City/County Management Association (2004), "Costa Rica Country Report Trends in Decentralization, Municipal Strengthening, and Citizen Participation in Central America, 1995–2003", https://icma.org/Documents/Document/Document/8519.

MIDEPLAN (2013), *Indice de desarrollo social,* http://www.mideplan.go.cr/component/content/category/249:indice-de-desarrollo-social-2013.html.

OECD (2015), *The Metropolitan Century: Understanding Urbanisation and its Consequences*, OECD Publishing, Paris, http://dx.doi.org/10.1787/9789264228733-en.

OECD (2014), *OECD Territorial Reviews: Colombia 2014*, OECD Publishing, Paris, http://dx.doi.org/10.1787/9789264224551-en.

OECD (2013), *OECD Investment Policy Reviews: Costa Rica 2013*, OECD Publishing, Paris, http://dx.doi.org/10.1787/9789264203952-en.

OECD (2012), "The case for future OECD Principles on Public Investment across Levels of Government", GOV/TDPC/RD(2012)5, OECD, Paris.

OECD (2010a), *OECD Territorial Policy Reviews: Sweden 2010*, OECD Publishing, Paris, http://dx.doi.org/10.1787/9789264081888-en.

OECD (2010b), *OECD Rural Development Policy Reviews: Québec, Canada 2010*, OECD Publishing, Paris, http://dx.doi.org/10.1787/9789264082151-en.

OECD (2006), *OECD Territorial Reviews: The Mesoamerican Region Southeastern Mexico and Central America 2006*, OECD Publishing, Paris, http://dx.doi.org/10.1787/9789264021921-en.

Paus, E. and K. Gallagher (2006), "The missing links between foreign investment and development: Lessons from Costa Rica and Mexico", *Global Development and Environment Institute Working Papers*, No. 06-01, Tufts University GDAE, www.ase.tufts.edu/gdae/Pubs/wp/06-01MissingLinks.pdf.

Peralta Quesada, L. and M. Solano Umanzor (2009), "Turismo rural comunitario como enfoque alternativo", Encuentros, *Revista Centroamericana de Ciencias Sociales*, Vol. 6, No. 2, pp. 135-162.

Trejos, J.D. (2008), "Basic social services: Achievements and bottlenecks since 1950", paper prepared for the UNRISD project "Public Policy and Poverty Reduction in Costa Rica", UNRISD, Geneva.

UNDP (2013), *Aprendiendo a Vivir Juntos: Convivencia y Desarrollo Humano en Costa Rica*, PNUD Costa Rica, San José, José, http://hdr.undp.org/sites/default/files/costa_rica_nhdr_2013.pdf.

World Bank (2006), *The Impact of Intel in Costa Rica – Nine Years after the Decision to Invest*, Investing in Development Series, The World Bank Group/Multilateral Investment Guarantee Agency, Washington, DC, www.wbginvestmentclimate.org/uploads/The%20Impact%20of%20Intel%20in%20Costa%20Rica.pdf.

# ORGANISATION FOR ECONOMIC CO-OPERATION AND DEVELOPMENT

The OECD is a unique forum where governments work together to address the economic, social and environmental challenges of globalisation. The OECD is also at the forefront of efforts to understand and to help governments respond to new developments and concerns, such as corporate governance, the information economy and the challenges of an ageing population. The Organisation provides a setting where governments can compare policy experiences, seek answers to common problems, identify good practice and work to co-ordinate domestic and international policies.

The OECD member countries are: Australia, Austria, Belgium, Canada, Chile, the Czech Republic, Denmark, Estonia, Finland, France, Germany, Greece, Hungary, Iceland, Ireland, Israel, Italy, Japan, Korea, Luxembourg, Mexico, the Netherlands, New Zealand, Norway, Poland, Portugal, the Slovak Republic, Slovenia, Spain, Sweden, Switzerland, Turkey, the United Kingdom and the United States. The European Union takes part in the work of the OECD.

OECD Publishing disseminates widely the results of the Organisation's statistics gathering and research on economic, social and environmental issues, as well as the conventions, guidelines and standards agreed by its members.

OECD PUBLISHING, 2, rue André-Pascal, 75775 PARIS CEDEX 16
(42 2015 20 1 P) ISBN 978-92-64-24698-0 – 2015-17

www.ingramcontent.com/pod-product-compliance
Ingram Content Group UK Ltd.
Pitfield, Milton Keynes, MK11 3LW, UK
UKHW051505290926
15471UKWH00008B/1421

9 789264 246980